DEPARTMENT OF HEALTH AND SOCIAL SECURITY

D1798602

National Health Service
The first thirty years
by Brian Abel-Smith

London: Her Majesty's Stationery Office

© Crown copyright 1978
First published 1978
Third Impression 1978

Government Bookshops
49 High Holborn, London WC1V 6HB
13a Castle Street, Edinburgh EH2 3AR
41 The Hayes, Cardiff CF1 1JW
Brazennose Street, Manchester M60 8AS
Southey House, Wine Street, Bristol BS1 2BQ
258 Broad Street, Birmingham B1 2HE
80 Chichester Street, Belfast BT1 4JY
*Government Publications are also available
through booksellers*

Cover picture: Cardiac arrest team.

ISBN 0 11 320249 0

Preface

This brief account of the first thirty years of the National Health Service in England and Wales is dedicated to all those who work in it or for it. Its main purpose is to describe, not to comment or explain. Perhaps this, apart from length, is the difference between an account and a history.

As the main readers are likely to be those to whom I dedicate this booklet, as well as those who are contemplating careers in the Service, a considerable emphasis has been given to developments in the organisation of the Service. Those who work in such a vast Service (the health service is Britain's largest employer) may wish to see an account of the whole of which they form a part—how it has evolved, how it came to be the way it is. The landmark of a thirtieth anniversary is a fitting occasion on which to celebrate the Service's achievements as well as to look ahead to what I have called in Chapter VI the unfinished business.

I wish to acknowledge the major contribution of present and past members of the Departments and others who have commented on this booklet in draft and supplied a considerable amount of the information. For the selection of the material and its presentation, I must alone take responsibility. Although I work part-time for the Government, any views expressed are not necessarily those of the Government.

BRIAN ABEL-SMITH
London School of Economics
Houghton Street
LONDON WC2

Contents

1 Health Care before the National Health Service

The National Health Service started on 5 July 1948. Britain was the first country in the world to offer free medical care to the whole population. Many other countries had developed compulsory health insurance schemes, but under them rights to health care were generally confined to those who had paid contributions and their dependants, and to pensioners. The principle of *universal* coverage for free medical care was entirely new. As Nye Bevan, the Minister who introduced the National Health Service, put it, "medical treatment and care . . . should be made available to rich and poor alike in accordance with medical need and by no other criteria".

The story of how we came to introduce the service and the prolonged debate about how the service should be organised has often been told. What is remarkable, is that the bold decision to have a national health service was taken in the middle of the Second World War. There was considerable controversy, for example, on such questions as whether it should really cover the whole population including the better off, whether dentistry and spectacles should be included from the start, and who should run the hospitals. But the Act to establish the Service was eventually passed in 1946.

Thirty years later, the older generation can remember from personal experience how health care was provided before the National Health Service opened its doors. The extent of the change can be appreciated by explaining what it was like before 1948.

National Health Insurance

Nearly half of the population was covered by the Lloyd George compulsory health insurance scheme which started in 1912 (under the 1911 Act). This gave the right to choose and use a general practitioner and to the free drugs he prescribed. By 1948, those covered were manual workers and other employees earning up to £420 a year. The scheme therefore excluded children, wives who did not go out to work, the self-employed, higher paid employees and many old people. Though some people belonged to insurance schemes on a voluntary basis, those who were not insured faced the prospect of paying both the doctor's bill and the cost of the medicines he prescribed.

Free health care was available to schoolchildren and to the poor from a district poor law doctor, or from a poor law institution, but people were very reluctant to face the Relieving Officer and the humiliating family means test which was required before services could be received. Many who could not afford to pay doctors' fees queued, often for several hours, at the so-called "casualty" departments of the voluntary (charitable) hospitals when what they needed was often the services of a general practitioner rather than a specialist.

Some general practitioners had separate waiting rooms for "panel" (health insurance) patients and private fee-paying patients, or would only see panel patients at lock-up surgeries while they treated private patients from their own homes. As the major part of the total earnings of general practitioners came from private patients, practitioners were heavily concentrated in the more affluent neighbourhoods. The poorer areas were sparsely served. For example, there were twice as many doctors per head in London as in South Wales. Four times the number of doctors per head lived in Bournemouth than in the industrial Midlands.

Dental and Ophthalmic Care

Before 1948, those covered by health insurance drew cash benefits for sickness or disablement not from the Government but from "Approved Societies"—most of them friendly societies. If, after paying out the statutory cash benefits, a friendly society had a financial surplus at its actuarial valuation, it could use it to provide its members with additional benefits. The main benefits provided were dental treatment and spectacles. About half the insured members were probably eligible for spectacles either free or with the member paying part of the cost. Spectacles were also provided by school ophthalmic clinics to children up to school-leaving age. The rest of the population had to buy their own. It was common for patients needing spectacles to go not to the optician but to a cheap chain store where they could try on spectacles until they found a pair which seemed to improve their sight.

In the case of dental care, the whole or much more often only a part of the approved cost of treatment was paid by those friendly societies which provided this additional benefit. Out of the 13 million people eligible for dental benefit only about 6–7 per cent claimed it in any given year. Dental care consisted to a large extent of removing teeth rather than filling them. Indeed, often teeth were extracted and full dentures provided instead. There was, moreover, a major shortage of dentists. There were few in rural areas and the time and expense of travelling to a dentist and the cost falling on the patient were major barriers to use. Apart from a few special units set up during the war, the dental services provided by hospitals were, except in the case of the teaching hospitals, very limited indeed. A survey of three Royal Ordnance factories in 1942 found that only 1 per cent of employees were dentally fit.

Local authorities provided limited dental treatment for expectant and nursing mothers and children under five, but the service could only reach a small proportion of those who needed it. Most authorities required the mother to pay towards the cost of dentures if she could reasonably be expected to do so. For every 100 mothers treated in 1945, there were 36 teeth filled and 316 extracted.

The School Dental Service had been set up in 1907 to give treatment to those children who could not obtain it in any other way, but its development had been slow and erratic. The service was administered by nearly 200 different local authorities and the extent of what they provided varied widely. The Education Act 1944 required local education authorities to provide dental inspections at appropriate intervals, and this was an important contribution to the dental health of children. But standards of dental care were generally low and most people attached little importance to caring for their teeth.

The Hospitals

Before the Second World War, the bulk of acute care in hospital and consultations with specialists were provided by the independent voluntary (charitable) hospitals which competed vigorously for charitable donations. Patients were expected to pay what they could afford unless they could show that they made regular contributions to one of the contributory schemes which helped to support the local hospitals or could obtain a "ticket" from a contributor.

The number, and the quality, of voluntary hospitals varied widely over the country. What could be provided in any particular area depended mainly on the donations of the living and the legacies of the dead rather than on any ascertained need for hospital services. The wealthier cities particularly London had hospitals, many of which were good by the standards of the time. But the smaller industrial towns were much less well provided and most of the hospitals were small. Few peripheral hospitals had proper facilities for X-rays, pathology or even surgery. The voluntary hospitals tended to pay low wages and salaries to staff—particularly to nursing staff. The nurses were expected to work long hours for their low pay.

The consultants and specialists were "honorary" and did their charitable work in the hospitals without payment for it. They depended for most of their incomes on payments for services to private patients. Thus doctors who limited their work to their specialty could only be found to work in hospitals if there was locally enough private practice to support them in their specialist work. Outside the main centres the hospitals were staffed by general practitioners or by doctors who were part specialist and part general practitioners. In the poorer parts of the country, particularly in Wales and the North of England, there were extremely few specialists because there were so few private patients. Those who were poor could only get good specialist care if they happened to be employed by or live near enough those who could afford to buy it.

With the outbreak of the Second World War, the Emergency Medical Service was established. The Government paid the voluntary hospitals to provide services—originally to air raid casualties but later to a wider category of people whose need for hospital care could be attributed to special war circumstances. Further financial support was given to the voluntary hospitals in the transitional period before the National Health Service was established.

To some extent gaps in the acute hospital services were filled by local authority hospitals. They provided the major part of the hospital obstetric services. Some counties and county boroughs had begun to develop acute hospital services after they took over the Poor Law Hospitals from the Poor Law Guardians under an Act of 1929. But the extent to which they did so varied according to the wealth and interest of the authority, the rates it was prepared to raise, and the priority it gave to this particular service. Patients who could afford to pay were charged on a means-tested basis, except in hospitals for infectious diseases, where charges could be waived. Local authority hospitals would normally only serve their own residents. Patients living on the wrong side of a county border would be refused admission even when there were empty beds. While some authorities, such as Birmingham City, Surrey, Middlesex and the London County Council made substantial progress in building up a good hospital system with specialists of high skill, other authorities made little use of their powers to do so. Their hospitals remained just as they had been under the Poor Law, according to a distinguished doctor—"ill-designed, deficient in sanitation, often isolated, bare, bleak and soulless".

The local authorities also provided the vast majority of hospital care for the chronic sick, for infectious diseases, mental illness and mental handicap. Over a tenth of the beds were for tuberculosis and other infectious diseases. They were also increasingly being made responsible for securing that arrangements were made for treating such conditions as cancer, venereal diseases and tuberculosis and for supplementing what the voluntary hospitals provided. The concentration of the voluntary hospitals on acute care meant that patients who did not respond to treatment were, after a period, transferred to a Poor Law infirmary for the chronic sick. The contrast in levels of staffing, in food, in the quality of the accommodation, and in the standard of nursing was often very great indeed. Local authorities were faced with a chronic shortage of trained nurses. Patients who were transferred inevitably felt that hope of recovery had been abandoned and that they had been put away to die.

In total, the local authorities provided about four-fifths of the hospital beds of all kinds in Britain but most of them provided types of health care which gave the doctors who worked in them on a whole-time or part-time salaried basis little prestige. Nationally there was a great shortage of hospital beds—particularly for certain cases. Cottage hospitals were often empty while large general hospitals had long waiting lists. Wales was particularly poorly served with hospitals. In South Wales, about half the hospital beds were in buildings which were judged, when they were taken over, to be too small or ill-equipped for their purpose. No general hospital of the requisite size and quality served the thinly-populated areas of North Wales.

Community Services

Several hundred different local authorities had the power but not the duty to care for expectant and nursing mothers and children under the age of five. To a widely varying extent, they provided ante-natal and post-natal clinics and welfare centres and employed health visitors to give advice in the home. Local authorities also either employed midwives or arranged for them to be provided by voluntary organisations. The majority of births took place at home usually with a midwife in charge, who would call a doctor if she thought it necessary. Although local authorities had the power to provide home nurses, this was limited to patients suffering from infectious diseases, expectant or nursing mothers or children under five suffering from various conditions. The majority of home nursing services were provided by voluntary district nursing associations financed by donations, payments from patients and grants from the local authorities. Domestic help services could until 1944 only be provided to maternity cases; from that year they could be provided to the sick and infirm. School children were inspected in schools and given dental, ophthalmic and orthopaedic treatment as well as treatment for minor ailments at school clinics. Before 1944 local authorities had to recover the cost from the parents unless they could not reasonably be expected to pay. From 1944, local authorities had a duty to see that free treatment was provided including in-patient treatment for schoolchildren and often for under-fives.

Ambulances were operated by a great variety of different agencies—individual hospitals, local authorities, the Red Cross, St John's Ambulance Brigade, police, factories and private operators. Payment had often to be made when the service was used. There was no co-ordinated system until the wartime civil defence service was established, and no guarantee that when an ambulance was desperately needed, one could be found.

The Money Barrier

Thus while free or partly free services of varying quality were available, there were serious shortages in many parts of the country. There was also a deep-seated reluctance to use the poor law services. The wives of working men in particular would often postpone going to the doctor or taking a child to a doctor because of the fear of a bill which could not be afforded and because of reluctance to ask for charity from the voluntary hospital. Often the compromise was to "ask the chemist". Many conditions got worse because of delay in seeking treatment.

Serious illness could also create financial catastrophes for middle-class patients. They might have to pay doctors' bills (both general practitioner and specialist), the cost of medicines and the cost of a nurse to look after them at home or the full cost of care in a nursing home. Private insurance schemes for middle-class patients were only just beginning to be developed. Moreover there was in most of the country a shortage of suitable hospital and nursing home facilities for paying patients.

The introduction of the national health services therefore relieved millions of the financial worry so often associated with illness. No longer did anyone need to delay in seeking health care because of the fear of running up bills they could not afford to pay. The main beneficiaries were housewives, children, the aged, middle-class patients and the self-employed.

But the service was created not just to make services free at point of use but to make them available wherever they were needed. It was designed to secure a much better geographical distribution of general practitioners, of specialists, of dentists and of opticians. Last but not least it was established to weld together an unco-ordinated series of hospitals of varying size, function and quality into an integrated and co-ordinated system designed to provide all needed forms of specialist care. The aim as stated in the original Act was "to secure improvement in the physical and mental health" of the nation's population "and the prevention, diagnosis and treatment of illness". According to one highly respected historian it was "the most unsordid act of British Social policy".

To enact a noble purpose was only a first step. The hard work of establishing the service had still to be begun. The buildings and trained manpower taken over on 5 July 1948 were far from adequate to realise the ambitious intentions of the legislation. Moreover the continuous advances in medical techniques and technology and the growing expectations of the public were to produce a continuing struggle to establish priorities for the use of limited resources. But what was important was that priorities within the Service were to be established on the basis of medical need rather than ability to pay.

2 The Early Years (1948 to 1960)

All that prospective patients were expected to do at the start of the Service was to register with a general practitioner, if they were not among the 19½ million already covered by national health insurance. By the end of 1948, 21½ million further people had done so. Doctors reported a marked increase in the demand for their services and many more patients were referred to hospital out-patients departments. Dentists and opticians were flooded with demands for service.

The introduction of the Service was a major administrative undertaking—particularly to establish the planned and co-ordinated hospital service. It also involved major changes in relationships—particularly for the medical profession—and it inevitably took time for all concerned to adjust themselves to the new situation. As set up in 1948, the National Health Service consisted of three different parts. First, there were the hospital and specialist services for which a new pattern of administration was created. Secondly, there were the family practitioner services which were separately administered—the general practitioners, the pharmaceutical service, the general dental service and the ophthalmic services outside hospitals. Thirdly, there were the services provided by the local authorities: maternity and child welfare, domiciliary midwifery, health visiting, home nursing, domestic help, vaccination and immunisation, prevention of illness, care and after care, ambulances, local mental health services and health centres.

The Organisation of the Hospitals

The biggest change made on 5 July 1948 was in the administration of the hospitals. The vast majority of the voluntary hospitals including all the teaching hospitals and all the local authority hospitals were transferred into national ownership. Over half the buildings taken over were more than fifty years old and most were poorly equipped for the practice of modern medicine even by the standards of that time. The Service began with 1,143 voluntary hospitals which provided about 90,000 beds and 1,545 municipal hospitals with about 390,000 beds of which 190,000 were in hospitals for mental illness and mental handicap and nearly 66,000 were still being administered under the Poor Law. The total number of national health service hospitals was therefore 2,688.

Boards of Governors directly responsible to the Minister were established to run the 36 teaching hospitals in England and Wales. The other hospitals were placed under the management of 388 hospital management committees. The planning of the hospital services and the employment of their senior medical and dental staff were made the responsibility of 14 Regional Hospital Boards. The Minister appointed the Chairmen and members of the Regional Hospital Boards and the Regional Boards appointed the chairmen and members of the hospital management committees in their region. All the members of boards and committees gave their services without payment.

The Regional Boards were established a year before the take-over and had to appoint their staffs from scratch. Their first task was to allot hospitals to management committees. A hospital management committee might be made responsible only for one large hospital or for ten or more hospitals of varying size. Separate hospital management committees were set up to run most of the mental illness hospitals or hospitals for the mentally handicapped. Apart from this it was normally intended that the hospitals grouped together under common management would be able to provide the main specialist and hospital services required by the physically ill in the district which the group of hospitals served.

On the establishment of the Service, a clear line had to be drawn between hospitals looking after chronically sick old people and homes for the elderly. The provision of the latter remained a local authority responsibility. Before 1948, many local authorities had provided for both needs in the same type of institution. Thus in many cases what were originally built as workhouse institutions had to be handed over to the predominant user. But part might still be used as a hospital and part as an old peoples home. No parallel division was made of institutions caring for the mentally ill or mentally handicapped. All their residents became hospital patients. Later it came to be recognised that many people in these institutions needed care of the kind local authorities rather than hospitals could provide. All who were in institutional care because of mental illness or mental handicap were regarded as hospital patients.

A sharper line was drawn between hospital medical practice and general practice. The important principle was established that, except in the case of accidents and emergencies, access to specialists should be only by the referral of the general practitioner. With the help of national finance, it was possible to employ doctors on a part-time or whole-time salary to work in hospitals who gave all of their time to specialist work, instead of having to continue to earn part of their livelihood from general practice. Thus whole-time specialists were appointed from existing and newly recruited doctors with specialist experience to work in hospitals which had previously relied on doctors who gave only part of their time to specialist work. One of the most important early benefits from the Service was that the main specialist services became available on a planned basis all over the country.

Decisions had also to be taken on the internal administration of hospitals. In the local authority tradition of administration, the chief executive of the hospital had been the medical superintendent to whom the matron was responsible, and also the clerk (except in matters of finance and building work where he was often directly responsible to the local authority). The voluntary hospitals had evolved towards a system of "tripartite" administration in which the Clerk or House Governor, the Matron and the Chairman of the Medical Staff Committee all had direct access to the Governing Body. It was this last pattern of administration which became increasingly applied under the National Health Service. As the medical superintendents of general hospitals retired, they were not replaced. Instead an elected representative of the medical staff became the formal channel of communication between the consultants and specialists and house committees and hospital management committees. Later this arrangement was also applied to hospitals for the mentally ill and mentally handicapped. The grouping of hospitals put the matrons of separate hospitals in an unfavourable position compared with the Group Secretary and the representative of the medical staff. Management committees and Boards of Governors were advised to invite a representative of the matrons to attend all their meetings.

On a more homely note, decisions had to be taken on what exchequer funds could and could not pay for. A circular sent to hospital authorities in 1948 made it clear that the Minister wished the tradition of Christmas festivities to be continued in the new service. Authorisation was given for up to five shillings per patient and resident member of staff to be spent on such festivities. A circular in the following year authorised the use of exchequer funds to provide personal necessities for patients—soap, toothpaste, razor blades, sanitary towels, a selection of newspapers, and in the case of long-stay patients toothbrushes, but not "cosmetics, permanent-waving, postage stamps, tobacco and sweets". "Committees and Boards should aim at achieving, in this field, a mean between austerity and luxury". A report from the Central Health Services Council in 1952 recommended that patients should have earphones rather than loudspeakers to listen to the radio, that meal times should be spaced to avoid long fasts and that patients should not be wakened earlier than 6 a.m.—and later if possible.

Of major importance for the staff of the hospitals was the establishment of the Whitley Councils to negotiate national terms of service. This was of special advantage to the staff of the voluntary hospitals who were brought into the new Service. Nursing and some other staff had generally had less favourable terms of service in voluntary hospitals than in local authority hospitals.

The Organisation of the Family Practitioner Services

The local administration of general medical practitioner services under the National Health Insurance had been undertaken by insurance committees—one for each county or county borough. A similar system was established under the National Health Service. A total of 138 Executive Councils were set up—eight of them covering the areas of two local authorities. The members were appointed by the Minister, the local authority and local professional committees. They were made responsible for administering not only the general practitioner and pharmaceutical services, both of which had been the responsibility of the old insurance committees, but also for the new general dental and ophthalmic services. General practitioners continued to "contract" to provide services for those patients they had accepted on their lists. They were free to take on what other work they chose. The representatives of general practitioners would not have accepted the position of being employees of the national health service. Dentists and those providing the ophthalmic service did not have lists of patients and had no obligation to provide a continuing service for any patient.

A Medical Practices Committee was established with the aim of securing a more even distribution of family doctors over the country. Doctors wishing to start in practice in a particular locality, or take over from a doctor who had retired or died, had to apply for the permission of this Committee. The Committee published lists of areas which were under-doctored, where permission would normally be granted immediately. But in an area which was over-doctored the Committee restricted entry. A maximum of 4,000 (plus 2,400 for a doctor with an assistant) was originally laid down for the number of patients on his list for which payment could be made.

In the early years of the Service general practitioners were dissatisfied with the level of payment. The dispute was resolved by adjudication in 1952. The adjudicator also decided that the "pool" out of which general practitioners were paid should in future be adjusted according to the number of doctors in the Service not as previously the population. This was accepted, and thereafter the Government put each year into the "pool" sufficient money to give the average practitioner the net income from all sources, including work for local authorities, which was intended.

After the award, the maximum list size was reduced to 3,500 (plus 2,000 extra for an assistant). At about the same time a special "loading" was built into the system of capitation payments. An extra payment was made for each person on a list between the 501st and the 1,500th and in partnerships the lists were averaged. In addition interest-free loans were offered to help doctors acquire premises for group practice. The aim of these changes was to discourage excessive lists of patients, to recognise that some practice expenses do not vary with list size, and to encourage doctors to work together in partnership or (preferably) groups. At the start of the health service, about half the general practitioners worked on their own but by 1960 the proportion of practitioners in partnerships of three or more had risen to 35 per cent.

The Local Authority Health Services

Local authorities were allowed to charge for domestic help services, arrangements for the prevention of illness (but not immunisation), care and after care and for supplies provided at residential and day nurseries. Half of the cost of the local health services were paid by the central government. The extent to which local authorities did develop services was limited by problems of recruiting staff and their willingness to meet half of the cost of the services. But the community care services provided by local authorities were the fastest growing part of the National Health Service during the nineteen-fifties (see Fig. 10).

The Cost of the Service

When, in 1946, the National Health Service Bill was presented to Parliament, it was estimated that the total net cost of the Service for England and Wales would be £110 million. At the end of 1947 the annual net cost was estimated at £179 million, but the actual cost for the first nine months was at an annual net rate of £242 million. For the second year (1949–50) the net cost, estimated at the end of 1948 at £228 million, turned out to be £305 million. These considerable underestimates of cost became a matter of heated political controversy. Winston Churchill, then leader of the Opposition, condemned one of the supplementary estimates needed for the Service as "the most wild miscalculations . . . an enormous addition to our expenditure brought about by the gravest carelessness" (*Hansard,* 10 February 1949, Col 536). In March 1950, the Chancellor of the Exchequer announced that a ceiling of £352 million (net) was to be imposed on the Service for the year 1950–51. Net expenditure in 1950–51 was £337 million and in 1951–52 £384 million.

As part of the policy of applying a ceiling to expenditure, charges for spectacles (other than children's glasses) and dentures were introduced from May 1951. Further and more extensive charges were introduced from June 1952 including a prescription charge and a charge of up to £1 for dental treatment from which there were exemptions for children and certain other categories. In April 1953 a Committee under the chairmanship of C. W. Guillebaud was appointed to examine the present and prospective cost of the National Health Service and advise how a rising charge could be avoided while maintaining an adequate service. The Committee's report published in early 1956 did much to allay public anxiety about cost. The Committee found that as a proportion of gross national product the current net cost of the Service had dropped from $3\frac{3}{4}$ per cent in 1949–50 to $3\frac{1}{4}$ per cent in 1953–54. The current net cost in real terms (in 1948–49 prices) was only £11 million greater in 1953–54 than in 1949–50 and changes in the size and age structure of the population meant that the real cost per head was almost exactly the same.

The early estimates of the cost of the Service had been far too low. But extremely little information had been available on what health care had actually cost before 1948. Moreover the estimates had had to be made before the levels of pay for many of those working in the Service had been settled. What was certainly not foreseen was the extent of the demand for dentures and spectacles which would face the Service when it started.

In the early years, the heavy expenditure on pharmaceuticals prescribed by general practitioners was frequently criticised. After the introduction of charges of 1s. (5p) per prescription *form* in 1952 there was a fall in the proportion of the cost of the National Health Service spent on this part of the Service. The charge was increased to 1s. (5p) per prescription *item* in 1956. But the gross cost—including the share paid by patients—rose between 1950 and 1957 faster than prices or average earnings. A Committee appointed to examine the subject in 1957 pointed out that the Health Service had been established at a time which coincided with "the discovery and large-scale production of valuable but expensive drugs". Indeed it was during the first twelve years of the Service that important developments were made in, for example, antibiotics, diuretics, steroids and psychotropics. Though the new drugs were costly, they provided major improvements in treatment. A whole series of measures was introduced to help doctors prescribe economically. For example, the profession agreed to limit the amount prescribed on any one prescription except in chronic cases. A Comprehensive Handbook on Prescribing was introduced. More visits were paid by departmental Regional Medical Officers to general practitioners to discuss prescribing costs.

The service to provide aids to the deaf was slow in getting started despite heavy demand. There were long waiting lists for aids in the early years. But by the end of 1956 over half a million Medresco aids had been issued. In this last year not only were over 180,000 new or repaired Medresco aids issued but also a total of 1,200 speaking tubes, ear trumpets and other non-electrical aids.

Financial Restraint

During its early years the dominating concern about cost limited the development of the Service. Not only were charges imposed and made more extensive, but expenditure was kept under tight control during the early nineteen-fifties. The impact on capital expenditure was particularly severe. Successive governments gave priority to the construction of houses and schools rather than hospitals. In the early years of the Service capital expenditure in real terms was at about a third of the level of 1938–39 despite the age of so many buildings which were taken over, the lack of new building after 1939 (except for temporary wartime structures), the overcrowding of hospitals for the mentally ill and mentally handicapped, and the acute shortage of accommodation for the chronic sick and for tuberculosis patients. The latter problem was so severe that some patients were sent to Switzerland for treatment. Very few complete new hospitals were built in the nineteen-fifties. Most of the capital expenditure which was authorised was used for modernisation and extension—for example, improved outpatients' accommodation, the provision of purpose-built operating theatres, increased facilities for X-ray and pathology, new boilers and extra accommodation for nursing and other staff—particularly at tuberculosis hospitals.

Not until 1955 did the government decide on a modest increase in the rate of expenditure on hospital building when it was decided to start some major hospital schemes and to make a special allocation for plant replacement and redeployment. The Minister, Mr Iain Macleod, gave high priority to relieving over-crowding in mental hospitals and

14

hospitals for the mentally handicapped by the construction of further wards and hospitals. In 1956–57 nearly a third of the total capital expenditure of Regional Hospital Boards was devoted to this type of hospital. By 1960, capital expenditure (United Kingdom) was running at a level more than 80 per cent greater in real terms than in 1949.

It had been envisaged that health centres would play a critical role in bringing together the three parts of the Service, but only nine new centres were opened during the nineteen-fifties. There was hesitation amongst the public. General practitioners themselves were suspicious of them. Were they going to lose their independence and come under the thumb of the local authorities which provided the health centres? Was this the thin end of the wedge leading to a salaried service? Lack of finance was, however, a major factor here also. Local authorities hesitated to build health centres because rents acceptable to general practitioners, who felt the money would come out of their own pockets, would far from cover the cost of the better facilities provided.

Tight control was exercised on hospital medical establishments— only in part because of limited finance. This led to fears in medical circles that Britain was training too many doctors and the medical schools reduced the number of students they admitted. A Committee was appointed in February 1955 to estimate the long-term demand for doctors and the consequential intake of medical schools. The Committee concluded that what was needed was a "reduction of student intake by about one-tenth, from as early a date as is practicable".

What the Committee had failed to identify was the extent to which British trained doctors were emigrating to North America, Australasia and elsewhere and the extent to which more doctors would be needed in the hospitals. In the light of later events, the decision to train fewer doctors was to have unfortunate effects. It was partly for this reason that the average size of general practitioners' lists which had been falling in the nineteen-fifties, started to increase from 1959. The number of general practitioners dropped by about 600 between 1963 and 1966. The Medical Practices Committee became less able to secure a more even geographical distribution of general practitioners and Britain became heavily dependent on immigrant doctors.

The Hospital Service
The problem of the shortage of accommodation, particularly for the chronic sick, tuberculosis patients, the mentally ill and the mentally handicapped was aggravated by persistent under-staffing. Between 1954 and 1960 over 5,000 additional beds were provided for mentally handicapped patients but this made no difference to waiting lists.

In the case of the chronic physically sick, shortage of accommodation continued to be a persistent problem, but as the need for accommodation for patients with tuberculosis declined, some of this accommodation could be converted for use by the chronic sick. Following a survey of services for the chronic sick and elderly in 1954–55, general hospitals were asked to ensure that they made sufficient provision for patients able to benefit from active geriatric treatment and rehabilitation. On the advice of a standing committee of the Central Health Services Council, criteria were established in 1951 to determine priorities for admission to hospital for child birth—adverse social conditions or for medical or obstetric reasons. It was expected that about half of the births would need to take place in hospital.

In the case of the mental illness hospitals, the number of patients rose until 1954 and then started to fall. This was the result of trends which had started much earlier. New forms of treatment were cutting lengths of stay. From the early nineteen-fifties certain hospitals greatly reduced restrictions and encouraged new attitudes to the care of patients. By 1954, new drugs had made it easier to control and relieve symptoms. And new non-physical and social ways of treating patients were spreading. Increasingly the functions of the hospitals were seen to be treatment and rehabilitation rather than care and control. More patients were treated without admission and it became much less common for patients to stay in hospital for long periods. Psychiatric units began to be established to treat the mentally ill in general hospitals near their own homes instead of at large distant specialist hospitals. Day hospitals were also started.

A Royal Commission re-examined the law governing patients with mental illness or mental handicap and on the basis of its report the Mental Health Act 1959 gave legislative support for the fundamental changes which were taking place. It led to the vast majority of patients being admitted to whatever hospital was appropriate without any legal formality. Moreover where compulsory powers had to be used, the decision to use them was taken by doctors and social workers: no longer were magistrates involved in such matters. In addition, a statutory direction under the Act made it a duty for local authorities to provide accommodation, training and day centres to care for the mentally ill and mentally handicapped outside hospital.

Doctors' Pay

In the second half of the nineteen-fifties relations between the Government and the medical profession again became strained over the question of doctors' pay. In early 1956 a claim was made by the profession for a cost of living increase but the Government told the profession in July that it was unwilling to consider the claim at that time. The Government finally conceded an interim payment and set up a Royal Commission in early 1957, to examine the whole question of doctors' and dentists' pay. This reported in early 1960 and recommended a considerable increase in remuneration which was paid retrospectively. A special review body, reporting direct to the Prime Minister, was established to advise on doctors' and dentists' pay in the future, as recommended by the Royal Commission.

Conclusion

By 1960, current expenditure on the Service in the United Kingdom was at a level over 30 per cent greater in real terms than in 1949, although capital and current expenditure in 1960 amounted to a slightly lower proportion of the gross domestic product in 1960 than in 1949 (see Figs. 1 and 2). Considerable progress had been made in expanding the services provided to patients during the nineteen-fifties. Falling demand and charges lowered the initial cost of the dental and ophthalmic services to public funds so that an increasing share of the national budget was available for the hospitals.

Out-patients attendances (including accidents and emergencies) rose from 36.1 million in 1949 to 41.7 million in 1960, and in-patients treated from 2.9 million to over 4.1 million (see Figs. 8 and 9). Waiting lists which had amounted to nearly 500,000 in 1949 had fallen to about 465,000 by 1960. In the surgical specialties the major developments were the consequences of improvements in anaesthetics and in care before and after operations. This made it possible for more operations to be performed safely on the frail and elderly. But the invention of new effective drugs and vaccines was undoubtedly the most significant area of medical advance. The local authorities expanded their services even more rapidly than the hospitals as manpower became available, though the rate of progress varied widely between different authorities.

It was during the early years of the National Health Service that diphtheria was virtually eliminated as a cause of death in children. By the late nineteen-fifties the same had become true of poliomyelitis. The death rate of mothers in childbirth dropped by nearly two-thirds and of children in the first year of life by over one-third. In 1960 the death rate from tuberculosis—still a major threat to the health of the nation in 1948—had dropped to one-seventh of the rate at the start of the Service. All this was a continuation of earlier trends, but the National Health Service had ensured that new developments in prevention, cure and care were made available to all.

Those responsible for managing the Service centrally, regionally and locally had had to learn as they went along. Inevitably mistakes were made. The main effort during the nineteen-fifties was devoted to managing the hospital services. Some of the grave shortages of accommodation which had faced the Service in its first few years had been alleviated. The number of people accommodated in mental illness hospitals was falling. The growing success in overcoming tuberculosis released hospital buildings for other uses. As the number of children needing hospital care fell, the space could be used for other purposes. Severe problems of overcrowding remained in the hospitals for the mentally handicapped and there was a continuing need to provide more accommodation, facilities and staff for the growing proportion of elderly. Some of these trends could be predicted by those managing the Service but not all. There had to be continuous adaptation in response to changing medical practice and changing needs—an ability to provide for the unexpected.

3 Growth and Development (1960 to 1974)

As Britain's economy recovered from the war, the debate about why the Service had cost more than originally estimated faded into political memory. Successive governments allocated a higher rate of growth of current expenditure to the Service, a major programme was launched to replace and upgrade old hospital buildings and from 1966 onwards health centres began to be constructed on a considerable scale.

The Hospitals

In early 1962 the Minister of Health, Mr Enoch Powell, published *The Hospital Plan*. This was to be the start of a ten-year "rolling" plan of hospital construction and attempted to lay down uniform criteria for the need for hospital care for the whole country. The plan recognised that many of the hospitals taken over in 1948 were in obsolete buildings. About 45 per cent of them were originally erected before 1891 and 21 per cent before 1861. Some were in the wrong place by modern standards. Even some hospitals built in the nineteen-thirties did not conform with modern principles of hospital planning.

A major hospital construction programme raised many questions: How many hospital beds should be built per thousand population? How large should a hospital be? What functions should be incorporated within a hospital to serve a district? The Hospital Plan gave tentative answers to these questions.

At the end of 1960 the number of acute beds per thousand population varied from three in the East Anglian Region to 5.6 in the Liverpool Region. In the light of local studies of the needs of particular areas, a ratio of 3.3 beds per thousand was established as the normal limit of requirements plus a national average of 0.58 beds per thousand for maternity cases. For geriatric patients a further 1.4 beds per thousand were estimated to be required as a national average. It was further estimated, on the trend then emerging, that mental illness beds would continue to drop from 3.3 to 1.8 per thousand by 1975. The requirement for beds for mentally handicapped patients was provisionally put at 1.3

per thousand.

The main hospital services were to be brought together in district general hospitals (normally of 600 to 800 beds) to serve a population of 100,000 to 150,000, which would provide the main acute services, a maternity unit, a geriatric unit, a short-stay psychiatric unit and facilities for infectious disease. It was however thought that some small maternity units and long-stay annexes should be retained in the smaller towns. Separate long-stay units for mental illness patients were also expected to be needed in the long run but they should not be too large or in isolated positions. The plan saw no place in the long run for many existing mental hospitals. For the mentally handicapped, separate hospitals of not more than 200 beds were envisaged.

A total of 90 new and 134 substantially remodelled hospitals was planned to be started by 1970–71. This proved to be over-ambitious. The cost of new hospital construction had been seriously underestimated. In 1966, Mr Powell's successor, Mr Kenneth Robinson, published a revised plan which, though more modest, was more costly. While Mr Powell had envisaged spending £500 million over ten years, Mr Robinson envisaged spending £1,000 million over ten years. By 1974, about a quarter of district general hospital beds were provided in new or substantially remodelled hospitals—a somewhat slower rate of progress than had been envisaged twelve years earlier. Nevertheless, the achievement was impressive. For example, a network of new District General Hospitals was firmly established in Wales. This network should be largely completed in the nineteen-eighties. The new hospitals provided not only better treatment facilities for patients but also improved working conditions for staff and amenities for patients. Most patients were accommodated in units of four or six and a considerable proportion of beds were in single rooms. Purpose-built day rooms were provided for patients who were up and about and bathroom facilities were greatly improved.

A Royal Commission on Medical Education was appointed in 1965 and issued an interim memorandum in 1966 which pointed out the urgent need to increase the number of medical students. Following the final report of the Commission in 1968, the Government announced plans to increase the number of students entering medical schools in Great Britain from 2,400 in 1965 to just over 4,000 by 1980. As a result, high priority was given to teaching hospitals in the hospital building programme. For example, in 1971 the first purpose-built and completely integrated teaching hospital and medical school in Britain was completed in Wales.

The Hospital Building Programme was implemented by the Regional

Hospital Boards and by the Boards of Governors of teaching hospitals. The regional architects and engineers planned some hospitals, but more often they commissioned private architects to work with them. As so little hospital building had been undertaken for over twenty years, British architects and engineers lacked experience and a visit was arranged to the United States to study recent developments. The Department produced guidance on how particular parts of hospitals could be efficiently and economically designed (hospital building notes) and on detailed aspects of design (hospital technical memoranda). It also launched a major programme of research and development in hospital planning.

By the mid-sixties it was becoming clear that the type of hospital which was being built—typically a tall building on a squat base "a matchbox on a muffin"—was costly to build, expensive to run, rather inflexible to use and not much liked by the public. An experimental low-rise hospital was designed at Greenwich by the Department with a particularly flexible arrangement of wards. This was followed by two "Best Buy" hospitals—at Frimley and Bury St Edmunds, which were designed to be economical to build and planned to be economical to run. The "Best Buy" hospital had a tender price about 60 per cent lower in real terms than hospitals built ten years earlier to serve similar populations. The "Best Buy" hospitals were built at a ratio of two acute beds per thousand. The Hospital Plan had made it clear that the recommended bed to population ratios had not taken account of the potential development of services outside hospital or of the scope for increased efficiency in the hospitals themselves. It was expected that the bed ratios might well be reduced later on. From 1975 the planning norm was reduced to 2.8 beds per thousand.

Apart from these "Best Buy" hospitals, each hospital project was, during the sixties, laboriously planned as a "one off" job. The process involved extensive consultation with those who were to use different parts of the hospital, some of whom would have retired before the hospital was built. The whole process was slow and costly, despite strong local pressures for new hospitals to be built. By the early nineteen-seventies, there were fears that the lengthy planning and design stage could become a bottleneck which would hold back the growth of the whole construction programme. To help resolve this problem, the Department collaborated with Regional Hospital Boards on the "Harness" concept—a kit of standard designs and plans for individual parts of hospital buildings which could be arranged on a "harness" of communications to form a complete hospital.

The Distribution of Hospital Revenue

The construction of new hospitals had an increasing impact on the distribution of money allotted for the hospital services. The initial distribution of money had been on the basis of what particular hospitals had spent before the Health Service was established and before financial controls were tightened. But this distribution became modified over the years after examination of the relative costs of different hospitals, their levels of staffing and the work they did. The general principle was to provide as a minimum the money needed to maintain existing services. Further money was provided to meet the extra costs of any new hospital buildings which were opened, caused by the higher quality and more intensive services which they were designed to provide. This benefited those regions which had the skills to press on rapidly with the construction of hospitals. It also benefited Wales where special efforts were made to improve and replace hospitals in view of the low quality of what had existed before 1948. Whatever further money was available was used to enable each hospital authority to undertake new developments: larger proportionate shares were given to those authorities whose needs seemed to be greatest. As the money needed to fund new hospital building increased, little was left over to try and help the under-provided parts of the country. Nevertheless, revenue allocations to regional hospital boards per head varied much less widely in 1971–72 than in 1950–51. In 1971–72 the best provided region received about a third more per head than the region with the lowest allocation per head. In 1950–51 the best provided region had received over twice the allocation per head of the worst provided region.

In 1969, the responsibility for the health services of Wales was transferred to the Secretary of State for Wales and the apportionment of funds between England and Wales was based on existing levels of expenditure.

A more objective method of allocating money to the English Regions was developed in 1970—this became known as the "Crossman formula" and was introduced from 1971–72. It was decided to abandon the system of giving extra revenue to Regional Hospital Boards for newly opened buildings to make hospital authorities consider more carefully the running costs of any new hospitals they built, as the extra costs would have to be found out of future allocations to the Region. It was decided to reduce steadily this special element of funding year by year until it was abolished at regional level from 1977–78. Half of the money allocated under the Crossman formula was based on the population served and a quarter each on the basis of the number of beds and the number of cases treated. It was decided to move in annual steps towards "fairness" as defined by the formula on the assumption that it would be reached over a period of ten years. Below regional level and in Wales the earlier method of allocation was retained until after the reorganisation of the Service in 1974.

The Family Doctor and Community Services

In 1962 local authorities were asked to produce ten-year plans for the development of their services. Their first plans published in 1963 showed wide variations in the extent to which different authorities intended to develop their services.

During the nineteen-sixties the local authority services became more closely co-ordinated with the family doctor services. A way was found of overcoming an important obstacle to co-ordination. As each general practitioner had his own list, patients living in a locality could be on the lists of several different doctors. On the other hand, each district nurse, home midwife or health visitor gave services only to those living in a geographically defined locality. Thus a nurse, midwife or health visitor might be in contact with the patients of many different doctors. This created problems of communication between doctors and nursing staff and prevented those in primary care from working together as a team.

From the middle fifties some medical officers of health started to attach health visitors and later district nurses to doctors' practices where they only provided services to patients on the practice's list. The practicability of this was greater when several family doctors worked together as a group. This new way of working grew rapidly so that by 1974 over three-quarters of general practitioners worked with district nurses and health visitors.

Meanwhile from 1966 a major change was introduced in the way family doctors were paid. It resulted from widespread dissatisfaction about the effects of the "pool" system of payment on remuneration for general practice. When in a particular year general practitioners earned exceptionally large payments from local authorities, less was available for distribution for work in general practice. Moreover, while the pool system protected doctors' incomes when the number of general practitioners was growing more rapidly than the population, it did not increase their incomes when the population was growing more rapidly than the number of family doctors, as began to happen in the nineteen-sixties. The doctors claimed that this resulted in extra work which justified extra pay. They demanded that the "pool" system should be abandoned.

This was agreed. But at the same time much more fundamental changes were negotiated, partly to create greater equity in the net income of individual doctors and partly to encourage improvements in the services provided. The pool contained an element for the expenses of practice which was distributed without regard to the expenses each practitioner actually incurred. The system benefited doctors who obtained cheap premises and managed without any paid help at all, while doctors who had good premises and employed staff had to find the cost themselves. While previously each doctor had had to pay for any staff he employed, in future it was agreed that 70 per cent of the salary (up to a maximum) of employing two staff per doctor would be reimbursed directly to the doctor on an individual basis. While previously the doctor had to pay the cost of his practice premises out of his gross earnings, rent (or the equivalent in the case of owner-occupied premises) and rates were in future reimbursed to individual practitioners. This was not only fairer for the doctor who practised in a high rent area, but it encouraged doctors to obtain better premises. Even more important it removed one of the main financial obstacles to practice in health centres, as the higher rents could be reimbursed. In addition, the General Practice Finance Corporation was set up in 1966 to make loans to general practitioners buying, building or improving premises.

The role of capitation payment was also substantially reduced. A flat rate allowance (originally £925) was introduced for any general practitioner with 1,000 patients on his or her list and a parallel allowance for continuing responsibility for patients out of normal hours. There were extra payments for practising in an unattractive area and to give incentives for group practice. Extra flat rate payments were also made according to length of service to those doctors who had attended requisite courses in Postgraduate education. Fees for night calls were introduced and a higher capitation payment for any patient over the age of 65. These were the principal changes negotiated as part of what came to be called "The Doctors' Charter". As a result less than half of what the doctor received came from capitation payments.

The consequences of the "Charter" negotiations were considerable. Doctors' surgeries improved. By the end of 1966 two-thirds of practices had claimed for ancillary staff. By 1974, most doctors had one or more supporting staff. This in turn encouraged many doctors to see national health service patients by appointment. It also probably led to more extensive records being kept and to records being consulted to a greater extent. It also encouraged general practitioners to employ surgery nurses to work with them. There was also a major expansion in postgraduate medical education and from the middle nineteen-sixties an increasing number of doctors who intended to enter general practice undertook planned vocational training.

The "Doctors' Charter" and the more favourable economic climate resulted in a rapid growth of health centres. At the end of 1965, only 30 health centres were open in the whole of England and Wales. By the end of 1973, 523 health centres were open (See Fig. 3). By 1974 about one doctor in seven worked in a health centre designed to accommodate the basic primary care team, including district nurses and health visitors: many others worked from other premises which had been adapted or built for working as a team. The maternity and child health services could thus be provided on the same premises as the primarily treatment services provided by family doctors. Both these types of development made it easier for those in primary care to work closely together. Home midwifery was, however, on the decline (See Fig. 6.) From the late nineteen-sixties the aim of policy was to make it possible for all births to take place in hospital. While in 1960, 34 per cent of confinements were at home, by 1974 only about six per cent took place at home (See Fig. 12). This was possible partly because of a continuation of the trend for mothers to be discharged earlier after the birth of their babies (a trend which many mothers welcomed) and partly because the fall in the birth rate made it possible for a higher proportion of births to take place in hospital. In many parts of the country there was by 1974 sufficient hospital accommodation for all births to take place in hospital. The major work of domiciliary midwives became antenatal care and the care of mothers after discharge from hospital.

Dental, Ophthalmic and Pharmaceutical Services

Once the initial backlog of demand had been met, the ophthalmic service settled down to a steady level of annual provision of about four to five million pairs of spectacles a year. From 1956, NHS lenses could be put in new private frames thus giving patients a wider choice. In 1971, flat-rate charges were replaced by broadly cost-related charges with a maximum of £3.50 for each lens. (Flat-rate charges were reintroduced from 1976.)

In the case of the general dental service the charges introduced from 1951 were deliberately geared to encourage restorative treatment rather than the supply of dentures. Children and others were exempt from the charges. The charges were increased for treatment (maximum £1 10s or £1.50) in 1968 and for dentures (maximum £6 5s or £6.25) in

1969. In 1971 the system of charges was changed to half the cost up to a maximum of £10. (From 1976, a system of charging similar to that operating before 1971 was introduced.)

By 1974 about 26 million courses of treatment (including emergencies) were being completed each year in the general dental service alone compared with $8\frac{1}{2}$ million courses in the year 1949–50. The pattern of dental work had changed dramatically. While in 1935 the national health insurance dentists were taking out more than six permanent teeth for every filling they completed, and in 1949 NHS dentists in the general dental service were still removing over two teeth for every filling, by 1976 nearly six fillings were inserted for every tooth extracted. In 1935 national health insurance dentists had completed about 16 fillings for every 10 full upper and lower dentures supplied, by 1976 44 fillings were inserted for every full set of dentures supplied. Many people had lost their natural teeth before the Health Service started and thus had no teeth of their own for the Health Service to look after. Indeed it was found twenty years after the Health Service had started that nearly half of those without natural teeth had lost them before 1948. The greatest increase in the use of the general dental service came from children. Leaving aside emergencies, the number of courses of treatment for children under 14 was multiplied about $15\frac{1}{2}$ times between 1949–50 and 1974, while adult courses were multiplied by about three and a half.

In the pharmaceutical service, charges were abolished in 1965, reintroduced in 1968 and increased in 1971.

Control of Medicines
Concern about the possible risks from new medicinal products following the thalidomide case led to an agreement with the pharmaceutical industry that new products would not be marketed without the approval of a central Committee on Safety of Drugs which started work in 1964. Control over the marketing of medicinal products was given a statutory basis under the Medicines Act 1968. From 1971 the function of giving approval for marketing was vested in the Health Ministers and from that date a statutory committee, the Committee on Safety of Medicines, the successor to the Committee on Safety of Drugs, has advised Ministers on the safety, quality and efficacy of new medicinal products.

Mental Illness and Mental Handicap
The number of patients resident in mental illness hospitals continued to fall close to the rate forecast in the Hospital Plan—from over

136,000 at the end of 1960 to less than 98,000 by the end of 1974 (See Fig 7). The number of in-patients per thousand had been forecast as 1.8 by 1975 in the Hospital Plan. The rate in that year was only slightly higher at 1.9. The number of admissions on the other hand rose from 115,000 in 1960 to 181,000 in 1974. Lengths of stay fell considerably so that by 1974 over 52 per cent of patients admitted stayed for less than a month, compared with 35 per cent in 1960. More psychiatric units had also been developed in general hospitals, though the adequacy and suitability of what was provided varied considerably. Out-patient attendances rose from about 1.1 in 1961 to over 1.4 million in 1974 and day patient attendance rose dramatically from about 300,000 in 1961 to over 2.8 million in 1974.

There was much less scope for short-stay admissions, day hospital or out-patient treatment in the case of the mentally handicapped. There was a slower fall in the number of persons accommodated during the nineteen-sixties and many of the hospitals continued to be seriously overcrowded. There was a steady change in the type of patient for whom care had to be provided. A lower proportion of the patients had mild handicap. In the past such patients had been available to help with the work of the hospitals; now they were more likely to be living with their families or in local authority accommodation. A higher proportion of the patients had severe mental and physical handicap and such patients survived to a greater age than had been the case in the past. The hospitals became more seriously under-staffed to provide their patients with the care they needed, let alone the proper stimulation, occupation and training. One reason for under-staffing was under-financing. But another was the difficulty of attracting staff to work in hospitals, many of which were very old and sited in isolated surroundings. In general the hospitals were large, badly furnished, under-staffed and some were poorly managed.

In the late nineteen-sixties public attention became focussed on the long stay hospitals as a result of allegations of the ill-treatment of patients and other failings. The reports of Committees of Inquiry, established to investigate these complaints, accepted the truth of a sufficient number of these allegations to stimulate a major re-orientation of priorities. The Secretary of State, Mr Richard Crossman, initiated a re-examination of standards of care in hospitals for the mentally ill and mentally handicapped. In 1969 he established the Hospital Advisory Service to visit long-stay hospitals and give advice locally on how to improve the management of patient care. Its Director also reported to the Secretary of State about conditions in particular hospitals. Teams from the Service visited the hospitals for the mentally handicapped, mentally ill and aged. Minimum standards were laid down for levels of medical, nursing and domestic staffing, expenditure on food, accommodation, and other facilities.

A White Paper on Better Services for the Mentally Handicapped was published in 1971 which contained a twenty year plan for repatterning the services on a local basis. Local authority residential places were to be multiplied by six and day centre places by three. As a result, the number of mentally handicapped people in hospital was to be virtually halved. No more large institutions were to be built. New localised hospital units of not more than 100 to 200 beds were to provide a highly specialised service for those who needed it, while purely residential needs were to be met in other ways. The key to the programme was joint planning between the hospital service and the local authorities. Meanwhile there was to be a continuing drive to improve the quality of life for mentally handicapped people living in hospital. Just as institutional provision for the aged had in 1948 been divided between welfare care which became the responsibility of local authorities and hospital care which became the responsibility of the National Health Service, a similar division needed to be steadily created in responsibility for those at present accommodated in the hospitals for the mentally handicapped. To achieve this a major extension was needed in the community care services provided by local authorities.

Community care for the mentally ill and mentally handicapped
Although the local authorities had, from 1959, been given a specific duty to provide community services for the mentally ill and mentally handicapped, the fulfilment of this duty was not given high priority. Faced with limited finance and often a lack of knowledge of what needed to be done, local authorities tended to give more attention to extending those services for which they were solely responsible than to developing community care services to take the place of hospital services for those who could manage in the community.

In the case of the mentally handicapped good progress was made in providing junior training centres (from 1970 special schools). Centres to provide training and occupation for adults were much less developed. By 1974, about half of the places estimated to be needed were provided. In the case of residential facilities, by 1974 about a third of the places estimated to be needed were provided. There were however still some local authorities which made no provision at all. The amount of social workers' time devoted to the mentally handicapped was seriously inadequate.

Provision for the mentally ill was still more deficient. In 1974 only about a sixth of the day centre places and a third of the residential care facilities estimated to be needed were available. In addition, community social work and other community services were seriously under-developed.

The Elderly

Although the proportion of elderly people in the population continued to increase between 1960 and 1974, there was little change in the number of hospital beds specifically provided for this section of the population. A much more active pattern of services was gradually being developed. More and more general hospitals established geriatric units to provide acute treatment and rehabilitation, where the aim was to enable the elderly to return to the community and prevent the need for long-term care in hospital. Day hospitals were increasingly established. From 1972 a special four year allocation of capital was made to improve the quality of accommodation for the elderly. Minimum standards of staffing and of other provisions were established in 1972.

The elderly, in particular, benefited from the expansion of the community nursing services. The number of district nurses in whole time equivalents rose from about 7,100 in 1960 to 11,700 in 1974. See Fig. 6. In 1974 2.3 million cases were attended of which about 45 per cent were persons over the age of 65. See Fig. 11.

Progress up to 1974

During the nineteen-sixties the scope of the National Health Service was widened. The original 1946 Act only allowed family planning advice and treatment to be provided when it was needed on medical grounds; and those who received appliances were charged for them. In 1966 Mr Kenneth Robinson asked local authorities to provide family planning services needed on medical grounds free of charge. From 1967, local authorities were given the power to provide services free for those who needed them for non-medical as well as for medical reasons.

The average daily number of patients in hospital fell from over 410,000 in 1960 to over 341,000 in 1974. However, the number of patients treated in hospital rose from about 4.1 million in 1960 to about 5.5 million in 1974. See Fig. 8. Waiting lists rose to about 550,000 in 1974 compared with about 465,000 in 1960. While the absolute number had risen, it had fallen as a proportion of the total of patients treated. The number of regular day patient attendances rose from about 2.6 million in 1970 to about 4.0 million in 1974. Total outpatient attendances (including accidents and emergencies) rose from about 42 million in 1960 to about 49 million in 1974. See Fig. 9.

Expenditure on the Health Service as a whole increased substantially. Capital expenditure in the United Kingdom rose from £24 million in 1949 to £162 million in 1974 in real terms. See Fig. 4. This was nearly seven times the level of 1949 and more than twice the level of 1938. By 1974, over 90 per cent more was being spent in real terms on running costs than in 1949, though a considerable part of this was needed to provide for the changing age structure of the population (particularly the increasing proportion of elderly people) and to allow for the reduction in the hours of work of staff. See Fig. 1. Total expenditure on the NHS capital and current had risen as a proportion of the U.K. gross domestic product from 3.8 per cent in 1960 to 5.3 per cent in 1974. See Fig. 2. Manpower working in the services increased from about 425,000 in 1949 (whole-time equivalents) to over 750,000 in 1974. See Fig. 5. If the Health Service were to be considered as a single employer, it would be the largest in the country. There were 15,000 more doctors working in hospitals, roughly 155,000 more hospital nursing and midwifery staff and 9,000 health visitors and district nurses. Despite the massive increase in expenditure, still more was needed. Not only were further developments required in services for community care, but hospital waiting lists remained a persistent problem.

But taken as a whole, the population was receiving a vastly better service than when the National Health Service started a quarter of a century earlier. For example, the risk of a mother dying in child birth was, by 1974, one-eighth of that in 1948. Deaths from diphtheria, polio, whooping cough and measles fell from 1,468 in 1948 to 33 in 1974. Nearly 22,000 people died from tuberculosis in 1948 and only about 1,200 in 1974. In 1949 about 22,000 hospital beds were used for infectious diseases; by 1974 only 2,900 beds were needed for this purpose. Some of this progress would have happened without the Health Service, but by no means all. The national service made it possible to exploit medical developments rapidly and made effective services including immunisation services available all over the country. It secured that specialist services were available throughout Wales and every part of England for the first time.

The period 1960 to 1974 was one of striking medical advances. Further important new drugs were introduced and surgical techniques, which had been developed earlier, were used more widely. For example, by 1974 around 21,500 hip replacement operations were being performed. High technology was introduced in the hospitals—open heart

Child nursing.

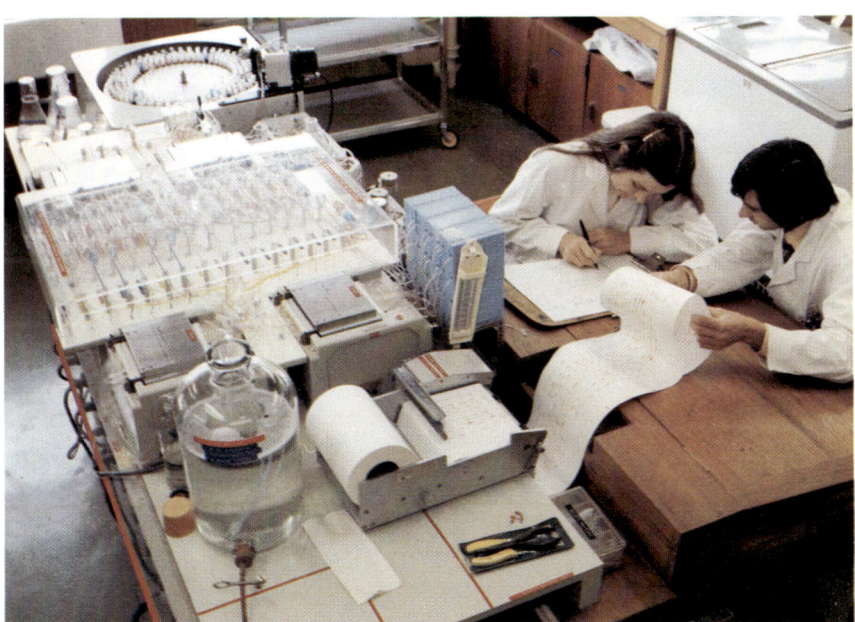

Blood-grouping in the laboratory.

Looking after the elderly.

Nursing mentally handicapped children.

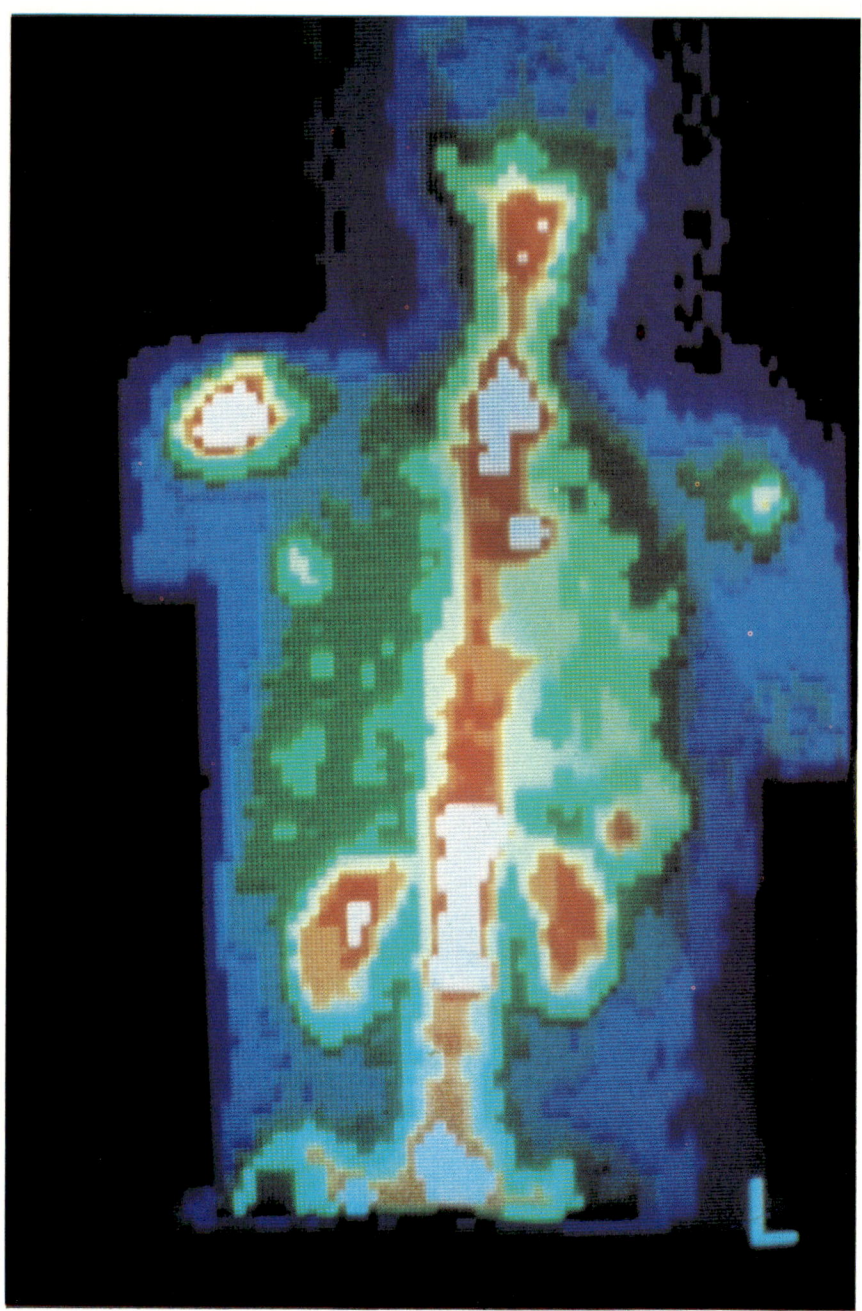

Computer processed isotope bone scanner.

surgery, cardiac pacemakers, intensive care units, heart lung machines and kidney machines which could be used in the home as well as the hospital. New diagnostic techniques using radio-isotopes and ultrasonics together with the British invented computerised axial tomography scanners, for the brain and more recently for the body, added new dimensions to diagnostic medicine. In the preventive field fetal and maternal monitoring services were introduced and it became possible to detect certain genetic and congenital defects before a child was born. Social changes were of no less significance. Changing attitudes towards the termination of pregnancy made an important contribution to the substantial fall in maternal deaths. Also of major social significance was the public acceptance of the woman's right to control her fertility and the development of new and effective methods of birth control—particularly "the pill".

Diagnostic pathology and radiology services within the National Health Service expanded enormously and have gradually been made available to virtually all general practitioners. There were about 4 times as many requests for pathology handled in 1974 as in 1949 and since 1949 the number of radiography points has trebled. The new technologies required the introduction into the hospital service of staff with a wide variety of skills. Moreover, it became essential for staff with different skills to work together as closely-knit teams. The National Health Service made it possible to create units at regional or supra regional level for highly specialised services such as infant cardiac surgery. Professional and technical staff (other than doctors and nurses) were the category of staff which grew most rapidly from under 13,000 (whole-time equivalents) in 1949 to nearly 40,000 in 1974. By 1974, the Service was employing 11,000 medical laboratory technicians, over 1,800 scientists, over 1,000 medical physics technicians, about 100 electronics technicians and about 100 artificial kidney assistants. Moreover, the role of nursing staff was steadily extended. For example they were increasingly monitoring life-supporting equipment in intensive therapy units and undertaking complex procedures both in hospitals and in the community.

Before the Health Service, there were no formal training arrangements for hospital administrators. By 1974, about 600 administrators had been trained under the National Training Scheme introduced from 1956 and in addition many locally based schemes had been introduced. From 1964 regular management courses were run. Important changes were made in local management. The medical staff of hospitals began to be organised in divisions based on broad medical or surgical categories to cope with the problems of management in the clinical field and examine how clinical resources could be used most effectively. Changes were also introduced in the management of the nursing services. Following the Salmon Report (1966), Chief Nursing Officers were appointed who were responsible for the nursing services in each group of hospitals. Parallel to this development was the appointment of Directors of Nursing Services responsible for the local authority nursing and midwifery services. Thus nurses had the right to be heard on all nursing matters and were made clearly responsible for planning and administtering nursing education and services. Nurse administrators were given further training to help them exercise their managerial responsibilities.

The life of the nurse became very different. Hours were shorter and the practice of requiring nurses to work split duties declined.

Working hours fell from a recommended 48 in 1949 (which was often exceeded particularly in the case of ward sisters and senior nursing staff) to 40 by 1972. Holidays were longer and equal pay was provided for male and female nurses. No longer could nursing staff be dismissed on marriage. While at the start of the Service it was rare for female nurses to be married, by the nineteen-seventies the majority were married. No longer were most nurses required to live in. In 1965 36 per cent of whole-time hospital nursing staff were resident. By 1975 the proportion had fallen to under 29 per cent. The regulation of hospital lodgings and homes increasingly became the responsibility of those who lived in them rather than of senior members of the nursing staff. The education and training of nurses became concentrated in fewer, larger, better staffed and better equipped schools. It was therefore possible to reduce the number of schools of Nursing from 878 in 1949 to 308 in 1974 despite the large increase in the number of basic learners. By 1974 there were 247 training schools for pupil enrolled nurses—most of them also part of the schools of Nursing.

In 1972 the Report of the Briggs Committee was published. Fundamental changes in the education and training of nurses were recommended. The essence of the proposal was that all those wishing to become nurses should undertake the same basic 18 months course of study on completion of which they could go on to registration level. Further study could lead to higher qualifications in specialist fields. It was also proposed that new statutory bodies should be set up to control the nursing, midwifery and health visiting professions and take responsibility for education and training. These recommendations were accepted in principle by the Government in 1974, but have still to be implemented.

The relative pay of junior doctors in hospital was greatly improved and a circular in 1972 laid it down that they should be entitled to off duty one day a week and on alternate nights and weekends. From 1969 extra payment was introduced after 102 hours of weekly duty and from 1974 after 80 hours. In 1948 the basic salary of a House Officer was (the lowest grade) £350–£450. In early 1978 the average salary was nearly £5,000. Their pay had multiplied by eleven times or more while that of the higher junior grades had risen by smaller amounts and the pay for a consultant on the maximum of the scale had multiplied by a little over four times.

At the same time the Service had in many ways become more responsive to human needs. Increasingly, volunteers came into hospitals to help with extras and keep up contacts with the outside world. The 200 Leagues of Hospital Friends supporting the voluntary hospitals in 1948 had grown to over 1,000 by 1974, bringing personal services such as hair-dressing and entertainment and raising funds for TV sets, mini-buses and social centres and adopting long-stay patients. Organisers of volunteers were increasingly appointed—particularly in hospitals for the mentally ill and mentally handicapped. Voluntary organisations and individuals also gave substantial services to help patients living in their own homes. Contributions and legacies were given to the "non-exchequer funds" of hospitals which were used for a whole variety of purposes. Not least was the critical service provided by blood doners who by 1974 were making a very personal gift to the health service of over 1.7 million donations of blood in 1974 compared with under half a million donations in 1949. The National Blood Transfusion Service through its network of centres was increasingly involved in processing these donations for ever more complex purposes such as special haemophilia treatments.

Husbands were welcomed to be present when their wives had babies and other children were allowed to visit their mothers. When young children had to go into hospital, visiting at flexible hours was strongly encouraged by the Central Health Services Council, and in many hospitals the mother could stay in hospital if she wished to do so. A survey of hospitals in 1952 had found that out of 1,235 hospitals, only 271 allowed daily visiting of children and 141 allowed visits only in emergencies. The opposition to daily visiting had been based on arguments that it "unsettled" the children or "caused them to be overfed". As late as 1962, an enquiry had shown that 750 hospitals did not allow daily visiting of adults. In primary care most general practitioners had appointment systems; nearly all had receptionists. There was less of a barrier between health personnel and users of the NHS. In these and other ways the Service of 1974 was very different from that of 1948.

4 The Reorganisation of the Service

As pointed out in Chapter 2, the Service had been established in three separate parts—the hospital and specialist services, the family practitioner services and the local authority services. There were, however, other health services which did not form part of the National Health Service at all—the school health service provided by local education authorities, the port health and other environmental health services provided by local government and the occupational health services provided by employers. As the Service progressed, the need for greater coordination of the health services was increasingly recognised.

The Guillebaud Committee which had reported on the cost of the Service in 1955 also examined its organisation. They concluded that it would be premature to propose any fundamental change in its structure but stressed the need for greater cooperation between the three parts. Particularly difficult problems of coordination were identified in the services for the aged. In the maternity services the problems were such that there was a need for a separate committee to be established to examine them. The Cranbrook Committee, which undertook this task, called for a clearer definition of the responsibilities of the different parts of the service.

The Porritt Committee

In 1962 a report by a non-governmental committee established by the medical profession and chaired by Sir Arthur Porritt was published. Its central recommendation was the unification of the Service under a series of Area Health Boards, though teaching hospitals were to be allowed to retain their own Boards of Governors with direct access to the Minister of Health. These new Area Boards were to take over the functions of local health authorities as well as responsibility for running the hospitals and the family practitioner services. They were also to be responsible for the school health service and environmental health services in industry and commerce. The Area Boards were to set up Regional Planning Committees to plan those services which needed to be provided over wider areas. Under each area health board there were to be four councils—one for each of the existing parts of the Service and one for occupational health services. The publication of this report made it clear that the unification of the three parts of the Service would be welcomed by the medical profession.

Problems of Co-ordination
One of the problems identified by the Guillebaud Committee—the maternity services—became less of a worry as the Service developed. The higher proportion of births which took place in hospital increased the role of the hospital maternity services and the growth of attachment and group practices and the wider development of health centres brought the community maternity and child welfare services closer together. But new problems were arising, such as early discharge schemes, where an integrated approach was needed. In the case of the aged, the closer co-ordination of the primary care services also eased the problems. But there remained difficulties in co-ordinating hospital provision for old people with homes for the elderly and the community health and welfare services provided by local authorities. There continued to be complaints that hospitals were accommodating old people who should be looked after in homes for the elderly and vice versa.

The case for unification grew as the services developed. The attachment of nursing staff to general practitioners made it seem increasingly anomalous that they were responsible to wholly different bodies. The nursing staff were employed by local health authorities and the general practitioners had their contracts with executive councils. Whether or not a general practitioner could have nursing staff attached to him was decided by a body with which he had no connection. Moreover, there were obvious problems where a doctor had on his list substantial numbers of patients living in different local authority areas. Which local authority should provide the nursing staff, and if it did, should the cost be shared between the different authorities?

As mentioned in Chapter 3, the construction of new district general hospitals raised the critical problem of how many acute beds per thousand were needed and the answer clearly depended to a considerable extent on the development of the community services. The more developed the nursing service and home help service, the greater the possibility of patients being adequately cared for at home. This could affect both the extent to which hospital admission was needed and how early patients could be discharged from hospital. Similarly, an extensive ambulance service was needed to develop day hospitals and day surgery to their full potential. This also influenced the extent to which in-patient accommodation was needed. Many years elapsed between the planning of a hospital and the time when it was ready to receive patients. The Regional Boards and Board of Governors whose task it was to build hospitals were in no position to control the future development of the community services provided by local authorities. Furthermore, more than one local authority might be providing services to substantial proportions of patients served by a particular district hospital. Costly capital construction could be saved by the development of community care services, but the separation of the services and their different boundaries of responsibility could frustrate rational planning of the hospital services.

The specific duty placed on local health authorities in 1959 to provide community care services for the mentally ill and mentally handicapped produced a further set of problems, as these services developed. In this area too, the requirements for hospital accommodation depended on the extent to which community care services were developed. In particular, the short staffed and overcrowded hospitals for the mentally handicapped desperately needed a rapid development of community services to lighten their load and provide more appropriate care for about half of their residents. But the Regional Boards and Hospital Management Committees could do no more than try to persuade local authorities to give these services greater priority. The problem of planning hospital services for the mentally ill and mentally handicapped was more formidable than in the case of the general hospitals because of the larger number of different local authority areas served in whole or part by a single large hospital. As concern about the standards of these hospitals grew, so did the case for pressing ahead with some form of reorganisation.

A divided service also frustrated the development of a clear rationale for the allocation of money to Regions and Hospital Management Committees, as the community health services and the teaching hospitals were separately administered.

On top of all this was the special problem of London. Not only was it carved up into parts of four hospital regions but the bulk of the Inner City acute services were provided by 12 undergraduate teaching hospitals and 14 postgraduate hospitals each of which had their own Boards of Governors. In the regions which had only one teaching hospital, the problems of concerting planning did not pose major problems. But in London they were formidable. Detailed decisions about the planning of London's hospitals had often to be taken at Ministry level.

There was thus a strong case for the health services to be brought together under a unified local administration. But how should health services be defined? Should they include the school health service, the port health service and the environmental health services? Should they include the welfare services provided by local authorities for the aged and others in view of the close relationship with hospital and community health services? If a line were to be drawn between health and welfare, on which side of the border should the home help service be placed? Some of these services had close relationships with other local government services such as housing. Should local government therefore be made responsible for the Health Service? Or were there special advantages in a health service planned and administered on a national basis? And if so, how could the principle of national accountability be combined with local democratic participation?

The 1968 Green Paper

In July 1968 the Minister of Health, Mr Kenneth Robinson, published a tentative Green Paper on the reorganisation of the Service just before the Seebohm Committee reported on the personal social services and a year before the Redcliffe Maud Commission reported on the reorganisation of local government in England. The Green Paper set out the advantages if the three parts of the Service were brought together under the control of 40 to 50 Area Boards which might also take over responsibility for port health and public health and whose officers might advise local authorities on their environmental services. The new Boards would replace the nearly 700 authorities involved in the existing services. Within the new organisation, Medical Officers of Health would be able to extend their role as community physicians—as specialists in community medicine.

The Green Paper left open the question of whether the new Area Boards would be committees of new local authorities which might be established following the Redcliffe Maud Report or would be responsible directly to the Minister of Health. It was however recognised that there would be advantages if Area Boards followed a broadly similar pattern to the local authorities. It also left open the precise dividing line between health and other social services.

The Seebohm Committee, which reported soon afterwards, had different ideas about the line which should be drawn between the Health Service and other social services. The Committee recommended that new Personal Social Services Departments should be established within local government which would take over some of the functions from local health authorities which the Green Paper had suggested might form part of the responsibilities of the Area Health Boards. The new Departments were to take over not only the children's services, and the welfare services which primarily served the aged, but also the care of the mentally ill and handicapped and the home help service which formed part of the local health services. This would mean a further reduction in the responsibilities of Medical Officers of Health following the loss of responsibility for local authority hospitals twenty years earlier. Medical Officers of Health had become concerned about their future before the Seebohm Committee reported and the Green Paper had suggested an important role for them in the new Area Health Boards.

In view of the clear advantages of bodies responsible for running unified health services having the same boundaries as local government, it is unfortunate that the Redcliffe Maud Commission's terms of reference did not require it to examine the implications for the Service of any local authority structure it recommended. Similarly, the pattern of local government in London had been established by 1966 on the recommendations of a Royal Commission which had, among other considerations, to take account of the scale appropriate for running the local authority health services, but did not have to take account of the scale appropriate for running hospitals let alone examine the catchment areas of existing hospitals.

When the Redcliffe Maud Commission finally reported in 1969, it recommended that outside London there should be 3 metropolitan authorities and within them 20 metropolitan district authorities. In the rest of England there should be 58 unitary authorities. The Commission did not conceal their view that the local government structure they proposed would be suitable to take over responsibility for the National Health Service.

The 1970 Green Paper
In 1970 Mr Richard Crossman, who had taken over as Secretary of State for Social Services, announced in a further Green Paper the firm decision that the National Health Service in England was to be administered not by local government but by about 90 Area Health Authorities responsible to the Secretary of State. In general the new Area Health Authorities would match the new unitary and metropolitan district authorities outside London proposed by the Redcliffe Maud Commission. It proposed that the new health authorities should consist of one-third of members appointed by the health professions, one-third appointed by the local authorities, and one-third plus the chairman appointed by the Secretary of State. Each area health authority should establish a Family Practitioner Committee to administer the family practitioner services run by the Executive Coun-

cils. Some 200 districts were envisaged to cover, wherever possible, the same geographical areas as the new unitary local authorities outside London.

In England the new health areas would contain populations varying from about 200,000 to about 1,300,000. While about a quarter of them corresponded to populations served by a district hospital, the remainder comprised more than one such district. It was therefore proposed that in the larger areas there should be committees for each district, consisting of a chairman and half the membership appointed by and drawn from the Area Health Authority and the other half drawn from people living or working in the district. At Regional level it was suggested that there should be 14 Regional health councils with some limited executive responsibilities but with the main task of advising the Secretary of State and the Area Health Authorities on the planning of the hospital and specialist services. The chain of authority would therefore run direct from the Secretary of State to the Area Health Authorities.

The Green Paper also announced the Government's decision on the borderline between the responsibilities of local government and the area authorities. Health Authorities were to be responsible for services where the main skill needed was that of the health professions, while the local authorities were to be responsible for the services where the main skill was social care or support. The case made by the Seebohm Committee for the new local authority Social Services Departments to take over responsibility for the home help service, and the community care of the mentally ill and mentally handicapped had been accepted. On the other hand, the school health service was to be a responsibility of the new Area Health Authorities as well as the remaining responsibilities of the local health authorities. From 1971, the new local authority Social Services Departments were established on the basis recommended by the Seebohm Report and the appropriate parts of the local health services were transferred to their control.

In Wales the health services had been made the responsibility of the Secretary of State for Wales, Mr George Thomas, in 1969. A Green Paper published in 1970 proposed that 7 Area Health Boards directly responsible to the Secretary of State should be established. The Areas would have district authorities similar to the district committees proposed for England but no regional board was to be created. Common services and technical services were to be provided on an all Wales basis where this would be economical.

The 1972 White Paper

After a change of Government, the new Secretary of State, Sir Keith

Joseph, issued a short consultation Document in May 1971 followed by a White Paper in August 1972 which set out the main lines upon which reorganisation finally took place in 1974. Instead of regional councils with mainly advisory functions, there were to be 14 Regional Health Authorities in a direct line relationship between the Secretary of State and the Area Health Authorities. Community Health Councils were to be established in each district to represent the views of consumers but there were to be no district committees. The White Paper also varied the composition of the Area Health Authorities. There was to be a lower proportion of local authority appointees. Except for the chairman who was to be selected and appointed by the Secretary of State and university nominees, the other members were to be appointed by the Regional Health Authority. Each Area Health Authority was to match a new county council or metropolitan district and, to encourage close collaboration, there were to be Joint Consultative Committees consisting of members of the two authorities to concert their plans and advise on services in spheres of common interest. With the unification of the Service, medical administrators working in the public health services and in the hospital service were to be brought together to play a major part in the planning and management of the Service at every level. As specialists in community medicine their tasks were to include assessing the need for health services, evaluating the effectiveness of services, helping to plan the best use of resources, developing preventive services and giving the necessary medical advice to local authorities on their related services.

A consultative document, published in February 1971, about the Reform of Local Government in Wales, had proposed that the whole of Wales be reorganised with seven county councils and 36 district councils and with the personal social services becoming a function of the county councils. The number of county councils—and consequently the number of area health authorities, whose areas matched those of the new counties—were subsequently increased to 8, their present total.

A consultative document and White Paper on health services, issued by the Secretary of State for Wales, proposed much the same organisation as in England, except that the Area Health Authorities, now to be increased to 8, would be directly responsible to the Secretary of State for Wales without the interposition of an intermediate all Wales authority. A Welsh Health Technical Services Organisation was to be created to provide certain technical services for the whole of the Health Service in Wales, including supplies, computer services and the design and development of large building projects.

The internal management arrangements for the new service were set out in what came to be called the "Grey Book" in England and the "Red Book" in Wales. Regional and Area Health Authorities were to be served by multi-disciplinary teams of officers. At the key operational level—the district—there were to be District Management Teams responsible in England not to the Area Team of Officers but to the Area Health Authority itself but in Wales the district teams were to be accountable through the area teams. District Management Teams were to consist of the Administrator, the Finance Officer, the District Nursing Officer and the Community Physician with a representative of the hospital medical staff and a representative of the general practitioners. Members of authorities were to concentrate on issues of policy and watch standards of performance and leave the implementation of policies to their officers.

Decisions had finally been taken on what services should be brought together to form the unified Service, on how the critical links should be formed between the health services and the related services provided by local government and on the new administrative structure and management arrangements. After the decision had been taken that the new local authorities should not be made responsible for the health services, the problems were how to create as close a partnership as possible between health and local authorities and how to find a balance between the ultimate accountability of the Secretaries of State for the planning and operation of the Service and the need for local democratic participation and involvement of consumers. What finally emerged was inevitably a compromise between conflicting interests—a somewhat cumbrous structure of regions, areas and districts—but each tier had responsibilities which needed to be undertaken.

5 The Lean Years following Reorganisation (1974-8)

On 1 April 1974, the re-organisation was put into effect. With the exception of the postgraduate hospitals, whose future was left for later decision, the health services, of which the school health service now formed a part, were brought together under the management of Area Health Authorities who were required to set up the Family Practitioner Committees to administer the contracts of general practitioners, dentists, pharmacists and opticians. The same Act which reorganised the Service also established a Health Service Commissioner to investigate complaints against health authorities—a proposal which had been floated in the 1968 Green Paper on reorganisation.

The Area Health Authorities in England were directly responsible to the Regional Health Authorities and they in turn were responsible to the Secretary of State for Social Services. In Wales, the Area Health Authorities were responsible direct to the Secretary of State for Wales (Mr John Morris). A change made by Mrs Barbara Castle, who took over as Secretary of State for Social Services just before re-organisation, was to increase the number of local authority members of health authorities.

It was now possible to plan and organise the services of each district on a comprehensive basis. This was the task of the multidisciplinary teams at each level of the Service. The vehicle was to be the new planning system. Priorities were to be identified through widespread discussion inside and outside the Service. The aim was to delegate more responsibility to health authorities without undermining the Secretary of State's accountability to Parliament for the money spent on the Service. The key to this was an objective basis for allocating money to health authorities.

There was now a common budget at each level of the Service. All nurses, both in hospital and in the community, were responsible to the District Nursing Officer. Attachments of nursing staff could be discussed with the Family Practitioner Committee on which the AHA was strongly represented. Representatives of the hospital medical staff and of the general practitioners played a full part in district management and professional advisory committees were established at each level of the Service. A unified administration had been created.

The Impact of Re-organisation

Careful preparations were made for the changeover, though the time-table was more rushed than in 1948 because of delay in the passing of necessary legislation through Parliament. The new authorities were set up by August 1973 and appointed their officers in readiness for the takeover. Intensive training courses were run for the key officers of the new authorities to help them appreciate the potentialities of a unified service. Senior staff, other than those working for postgraduate hospitals, had to compete for new jobs with the new authorities. Older staff were offered favourable terms for early retirement. A Staff Commission was established to safeguard the interests of staff during the period of reorganisation.

The transfer of responsibility took place Hemarkably smoothly, but it inevitably took time for new working relationships to be established and for all concerned to become accustomed to new ways of working. In multi-district areas, the change was particularly great. No longer were there members of management committees and Boards of Governors who could readily be approached when problems needed to be resolved. The teaching hospitals in particular had to adjust themselves to channelling their important proposals through Area and Region rather than approaching the Department direct. The establishment of teams of officers at Regional and Area levels and of management teams at district level was a development to which all concerned had to become accustomed. The important part played by nursing administrators carried further the developments in the management responsibilities of nurses which had followed the Salmon and Mayston Reports. They became full members of the teams of officers at each level of the Service.

The new regional health authorities had also to establish community health councils for each district to represent the interests of users. These important new statutory bodies had the tasks of advising management, making recommendations for improvements, and generally keeping an eye on the local health services. They had the right to be consulted on any proposals for important changes in services or major developments. In the case of closures or changes of use of health premises, as the result of guidance to health authorities issued in the spring of 1974, health authorities could only implement proposals if they agreed. Otherwise the proposals went to the Secretary of State for decision. It took time for all the CHCs to be established and in August 1977 an Association of Community Health Councils was set up at the request of a majority of the Councils.

Change is always more acceptable when it can be cushioned with extra resources. Inevitably those working in the Service tended to judge the initial success of re-organisation by whether it brought extra resources rather than by whether better use could be made of resources already available. It was therefore unfortunate for the reception of re-organisation that it took place only a few months after the "Oil Crisis" which led to decisions to cut public expenditure. Re-organisation tended to be blamed for what was largely the changed economic fortunes of the country.

On top of all this, reorganisation came at a time when successive pay policies had caused the pay of those working in the public sector to fall seriously behind that of those working in the private sector. With the ending of pay restraint, there was considerable unrest among NHS staff and fundamental re-adjustments were made in NHS pay in 1974–5. In the case of nurses and the professions supplementary to medicine, an independent committee under Lord Halsbury was asked to make recommendations. The magnitude of the adjustment can be shown from the fact that nurses' pay, for instance, increased on average by 51 per cent in the course of a year. The NHS is a labour-intensive organisation and these increases in pay were largely responsible for a substantial rise in the proportion of national resources spent on it. While in 1973, 4.7 per cent of the gross domestic product was spent on the cost of the National Health Service in the United Kingdom, by 1976 the proportion had risen to 5.7 per cent. See Fig. 2.

Thus reorganisation was followed by a period during which a whole host of factors combined to lower the morale of those working in the Service. Some of the problems were reflections in the Health Service of the national economic situation. But others were the culmination of trends which had been developing over a long period—the more active role of the trade unions and the conflicting interests of different professional groups which seemed to challenge long established conventions and relations of authority. Inevitably there were difficulties in adjusting to such fundamental changes. In his report *"Making Whitley Work"* published in 1976, Lord McCarthy dealt with some aspects of these problems and made recommendations for more effective consultation between management and staff in the NHS, and for the more effective representation of management and staff in the Whitley Councils.

Further acrimony resulted from the Government's decision to phase pay beds out of the National Health Service, changing the arrangements made under the 1946 Act by which hospitals could set aside private wards for patients willing to pay the full cost of their accommodation and treatment. This policy was supported by the Health Service trade unions and resisted by the medical profession. When towards the end of 1974, discussions of a new contract for consultants broke down, there was a restriction in the services offered by consultants and specialists. And for a period in 1975 junior doctors restricted their work to emergencies because of discontent about the delay in introducing changes in their remuneration.

The number of new outpatients seen fell by about 900,000 in 1975 compared with the preceding year or by a million compared with 1972. The number of main operations performed in hospitals (other than psychiatric) fell by over $\frac{1}{4}$ million between 1974 and 1975. Waiting lists rose by about 70,000 between the end of 1974 and the end of 1975.

Primary Care
The rapid expansion of Health Centres continued after reorganisation. Between the end of 1973 and the end of 1976, the number of doctors working in health centres increased by about 40 per cent. By the last year there were 789 health centres in operation (see Fig. 3). Under an Act passed in late 1976, doctors entering general practice in the National Health Service could be required to have vocational training. This was a major step towards the establishment of general practice as a specialty in its own right.

A New Emphasis on Prevention
A discussion document *Prevention and Health: Everybody's Business* was issued in 1976 as the start of a major campaign to encourage preventive action. Its main message was that, while the National Health Service could provide health services, it could not provide health. The main causes of ill health lay in the environment and in how people lived—in their life styles. Better health depended on people improving their lifestyle by, for example, abandoning cigarette smoking, drinking only in moderation, improving their diet and avoiding becoming overweight. Further papers continue to be issued on particular aspects of health. £$\frac{1}{2}$ million a year was especially earmarked to help health authorities to set up schemes for the fluoridation of water. An extra £1 million was allocated to the Health Education Council which enabled the Council to help launch a "Better Health" campaign, a regional campaign against alcoholism and provide more training for

health education officers. The number of health education officers working in health authorities was increased substantially.

The Act of 1973 which reorganised the Service included provision for a comprehensive family planning service. From April 1974 the new health authorities became responsible for both the clinics run by the local authorities and those run by the Family Planning Association. During the discussion of the Bill in Parliament there had been a long debate on whether or not this service should be provided free of charge. In 1974, the new Government decided that the family planning service should be free. From July 1975, free family planning services for women were also provided by general practitioners.

The Capital Programme

Although more hospital beds in new or modernised hospitals were opened in England in the year 1974–75 than in any year before or since, the future capital programme had to be severely cut. When firm decisions were taken by the Government about the level of capital expenditure, plans for building new hospitals all over the country which had been confidently expected to start over the next few years had to be abandoned. One consequence of this was that if whole hospitals were built with the remaining capital, particular districts would be favoured and this would delay the time when other districts could expect any substantial new building. This combined with doubts about the wisdom of building very large hospitals and the fact that no-one could predict with any degree of certainty hospital requirements ten or twenty years ahead led to the abandonment of "Harness" and its replacement by the "Nucleus" concept—a hospital small to start with, but which could be expanded later on. The "Nucleus" hospital, like "Harness," was based upon a kit of standardised departments using the lessons learnt from "Best Buy" as well as from "Harness" plans. The "Nucleus" consisted of about 300 beds which was a manageable size for building contract work. Work started on the first "Nucleus" hospital in early 1978. "Nucleus" designs were expected to be used for twenty hospital projects in England and four in Wales planned to be started up to 1983.

Until 1974, there had been considerable vagueness about what sort of hospital provision there should be for the physically ill other than that provided at district general hospitals. In that year, the concept of the community hospital was defined. It was envisaged that community hospitals might vary in size from 50 to 150 beds and serve a population of 30,000 to 100,000, although community hospitals in the more sparsely populated parts of Wales would probably need to be smaller than this. The day-to-day medical care would be provided by general practitioners and there were to be strong links with the community. The hospital would be used by a wide range of patients, particularly elderly patients who did not need the facilities of the district general hospital. It was envisaged that many community hospitals could be provided by the adaptation of existing hospitals.

Better Services for the Mentally Ill

In 1975, a comprehensive long-term programme to improve the quality of services for the mentally ill was set out in a White Paper. The core of the programme was a shift of care and treatment services into local communities. It advocated the development in each district, through the co-ordinated efforts of health and local authorities, of a whole network of health and social services which were to be used as flexibly as possible. The services were to include a general hospital psychiatric unit, services for the elderly severely mentally infirm in community hospitals, community psychiatric nursing services, day hospitals and outpatient services, day centres and homes and hostels in the community. Housing and employment services were also to be closely involved.

As these networks developed, they were to replace the services provided by the old large hospitals. The White Paper emphasised the complexity of the task, the need to maintain morale in existing hospitals, and the importance of careful and joint planning. Though no specific time programme was given for the plan, a 20–30 year timescale was envisaged. The annual levels of capital and revenue expenditure needed to establish the new pattern of services were estimated on this basis.

Planning New Priorities

Because of the economic crisis, the Service had to adjust to a lower rate of real growth of current expenditure of around $1\frac{1}{2}$ per cent a year rather than the average rate of over $3\frac{1}{2}$ per cent which the Service had enjoyed in the period 1970–73. This rate of growth was not much more than was needed to meet the needs of demographic change—particularly the rising proportion of aged in the population. But expenditure on many other services was being cut.

The common management of the integrated Service at regional, area and district level enabled resources to be transferred between hospital and community services and between the needs of different types of user such as the old, the acute sick, children, the mentally ill and the mentally handicapped. The mechanism for choosing a better allocation of resources was the planning system. When the Service had settled down after reorganisation and the Government could see far enough ahead the level of resources which could be allocated to the National Health Service, the new planning system was introduced —a unique experiment in partnership between central government and statutory regional and area authorities. The health authorities had been given the responsibility to plan and manage but to operate within policies and to respond to the priorities established by the Secretaries of State.

The process was started by a consultative document *Priorities in the Health and Personal Social Services* issued by Mrs Barbara Castle in March 1976 and a comparable document for Wales issued by Mr John Morris. The aim had always been that the annual planning cycle would involve all levels of the Service. In England the priorities, as seen by the district, would contribute to planning at area and regional level: these would in turn be channelled to the Secretary of State who would issue guidelines setting out broad national priorities which were to be interpreted locally in the light of local circumstances and taken into account by Regional Health Authorities in their own future planning and in the guidance they gave within their regions. As the first guidance was given before health authorities had made their views known, the document was consultative. Planning in Wales was to be on a similar basis, allowing for the different organisation. The main thrust of the plans in both England and Wales was to give a much greater emphasis to preventive services and to community care. Priority was given to the development of services for mentally ill, mentally handicapped, the physically handicapped, aged and children. As a result the rate of growth of expenditure on the acute services would be slower than for the services as a whole. Expenditure on maternity services would decline because of the drop in the birth rate. A major emphasis was put on the scope for rationalisation of the acute services through a reduction in the length of stay, a wider use of day care, and the avoidance of unnecessary admission. This would enable a number of small hospitals to be closed to release resources for developments within the acute services as well as in the priority sectors.

These priorities were broadly accepted within the Service, though there was criticism of the drop of expenditure on the maternity services and doubts about whether the switch in resources could be achieved to the extent indicated in view of the limited growth rate of revenue for the Service as a whole. Revised guidance, *The Way Forward*, was issued in England in September 1977. This stressed that the key to achieving the planned switch in resources was to be found in getting better value out of money already allocated. Illustrations were given of the way in which this might be done. In Wales the planning guidance was also broadly confirmed.

Collaboration with the Local Authorities

Reorganisation had brought the different parts of the health services under common management at the local level, but the key social services which could reduce the need for health services were the responsibility of the local authorities. Indeed the home help service and the domiciliary care of the mentally ill and mentally handicapped had been transferred to the local authority Social Services Department. Collaboration between health and local authorities was vital for effective planning. Local authorities and their matching health authorities were therefore required to set up joint consultative committees of members of both authorities. In particular, the success of plans for the mentally ill and mentally handicapped depended upon the willingness and ability of local authorities to expand their community services. To encourage collaboration, health and local authorities were advised to set up Joint Care Planning Teams to consider the needs of various groups such as the elderly, for both health and social services care.

In addition a special allocation of money was set aside from the NHS budget to enable health authorities to contribute to local authority schemes which would help those not requiring hospital care to be looked after in the community and thus to reduce the pressure on hospital beds. This system of joint financing was introduced from the year 1976–77 with an allocation of £8 million in England. By 1978–79 the allocation had risen to £32 million. In Wales, Area Health Authorities were given discretion to use their ordinary funds for these purposes and a central reserve was created on which they could draw from 1978–79.

Geographical Equity

The unification of the Health Service made it possible to introduce a more rational basis for allocating money to regions and from regions to areas and districts. The 1970 Green Paper had included a statement that in the long run financial allocations would be based on population served, differences in morbidity, the state of the capital plant and the special needs of teaching and research. A working party was set up in 1975 (The Resource Allocation Working Party) to recommend how allocations should be made to Regions, Areas and Districts. In its interim report the working party recommended a method of setting target allocations for regions for 1976–77 based partly on the number of cases treated by the hospitals of each region, but mainly on weighted population with special allowances for the service consequences of teaching responsibilities. A substantial move towards these target allocations was made in 1976–77—the last year when special allocations were made to regions for the running costs of new buildings. The system brought special help to the deprived regions.

In its final report, the Working Party recommended that revenue allocations should be made on the basis of population served, with weightings reflecting primarily variations in the use of services by different age and sex groups and certain variations in mortality ratios, with the retention of a special allocation to recognise the necessary service costs arising from undergraduate medical teaching. A substantial step towards this system of allocation was made from 1977–78. Mr David Ennals, who had taken over as Secretary of State, decided that the most deprived regions should be allowed a growth of revenue of 3 per cent and the best endowed region of only $\frac{1}{4}$ per cent. It was planned to progress year by year towards the new basis of allocating money defined by the working party. Similar principles were to be applied by Regions in allocating money to Areas and Districts.

In Wales, a Working Group on Resource Allocations was set up in 1974 to examine methods of resource allocation to Welsh health authorities. The Group produced its first report in December 1974 and a second in December 1975. It was then superseded by a Steering Committee on Resource Allocations which has produced two further annual reports. The population weighted formula for resource distribution, first produced in 1974, was refined each year. It differed in certain minor ways from that recommended by the English Resource Allocation Working Party. Allocations made by the Secretary of State for Wales were based on the advice of the Committee.

The introduction of objective, if in England somewhat controversial, systems for allocating money within the Health Service was an important step towards making a reality of "planning". While previously planning had often been seen in the Service as an attempt to find good reasons for claiming more resources, planning became accepted as a process of working out how best to spend a given level of resources expected to be available over the planning period.

50

Rationalisation of the Hospital Services

Thus the Service was faced with three different types of financial pressure. First was the pressure to shift resources towards the chosen priorities. Second, was the pressure to move towards a fairer geographical distribution of resources. Third, was the need to make extra financial provision for improved services provided in new hospitals as they opened. A total of about 21,000 new beds were opened from April 1974 to the end of March 1977. Health authorities were thus under the strongest pressure to rationalise their services. Hospitals which were no longer required were closed. While in the early years of the NHS the problem had been a shortage of accommodation, in the middle nineteen-seventies the problems were more accommodation than could be staffed and financed and hospitals no longer needed because of movements in population and extra provision nearer where people lived. Some bed closures were the direct or indirect consequences of new construction schemes, some of population movements (particularly the fall in Inner London's population of a million in a period of only ten years), some were due to changes in need (for example the continuing fall in beds for mental illness patients). In most cases formal closure proposals were approved by the relevant Community Health Council. In 1976 there were 22,000 fewer beds than in 1973. This compares with a net decline of 19,000 in the whole period 1949 to 1973 See Fig. 7.

Thus despite limited resources, progress was being made towards the achievement of the fundamental purposes of reorganisation. The process of securing a more even geographical distribution of services was being carried further and extra resources were being directed towards the priority services. Hospital services were being rationalised and the community services were being strengthened. Those who stood to gain most from reorganisation were patients living in parts of the country with poorly financed services and low standards of health and those who needed to use those services which had been given priority for development.

6 Unfinished Business

In the first 30 years of its history, the National Health Service will have treated about 135 million hospital in-patients and handled about 1,300 million attendances of out-patients (including accidents and emergencies). It will have received about 35 million donations of blood, supplied about 7,300 million prescriptions, provided nearly 500 million courses of dental treatment (including emergencies) and given about 180 million sight tests. But the aim of the National Health Service is not to provide hospitals or health centres, doctors or nurses, drugs or surgery but to improve health. And it cannot do it alone. Much depends on the environment in which people live. For example housing, work, cash benefits and facilities for recreation can all contribute to the improvement of health standards. Possibly more important is how people live their lives—the extent to which they harm their own health.

Standards of Health
In general, death rates in England and Wales are lower than those of most advanced countries. But deaths from lung cancer and bronchitis are high by international standards. Infant mortality rates have been falling at an increasing rate but not as fast as in some other countries. England and Wales have been overtaken in the last decade by Japan, France and Canada; and most Northern European countries have for a long time had a better record in this respect. But national rates are averages which conceal wide variations within countries as well as between countries. Despite 30 years of the National Health Service, mortality rates are in general a third higher in Wales than in East Anglia. Most worrying of all, despite 30 years of the "welfare state," the differences in mortality rates between social classes, are if anything getting wider rather than narrower. These are the problems which need intensive investigation and remedial action in whatever field such action can be effective.

But death rates do not tell the whole story. There is also a growing proportion of people with serious disability—caused in part by the earlier success of health services in saving life. Nor is this confined to the growing proportion of elderly in the population. More young people survive with serious disability—some disabled from birth, some the victims of disease and some of accidents—particularly on the roads. About three people per thousand are severely mentally handicapped. On average, one person in ten consults a general practitioner about a mental health problem every year. In the Greater London area alone, over 20,000 (mainly young people) a year are treated who have taken an overdose of drugs or have other drug poisoning.

Constantly Growing Demand

Faced with an ageing population, the health and related personal social services have to grow to stand still. Thirty years ago one person in thirty was 75 or over. Now one person in 20 is of this age. As working hours for staff are cut, and rightly cut, more staff are needed to provide a 24 hour service. Over the last 30 years for this reason alone, it has been necessary to employ many more nursing staff in hospitals. In general, medical advances require more staff not less to man new diagnostic equipment or help administer new treatments. For these and other reasons, although spending on the Health Service has doubled in real terms in the space of 30 years, there is still much which needs to be done. Modern medicine helps more people to live full lives, but it is costly.

Replacing Old Buildings

Compared to some other advanced countries, particularly those that have enjoyed higher rates of growth, the task of renewing hospitals or replacing them with more appropriate places of care was started late. While only about a third of the district general hospitals are in new or substantially remodelled buildings, a third of the present hospital stock was built before 1900. The task of providing the type of community hospitals which are currently envisaged has hardly begun. Most of the hospitals for the mentally ill are in unsuitable nineteenth-century buildings remote from the communities they serve and built to provide custody and asylum rather than therapy or care. Most of the hospital accommodation for the mentally handicapped is too old, too large and too institutional. Much of the accommodation for the elderly is in unsuitable buildings converted from other uses. While considerable progress has been made in providing buildings for primary care in which preventive and curative services can work together in tandem, much still remains to be done—particularly in the inner city areas.

The Acute Services

In the acute services the urgent need is to reduce the time spent waiting for hospital treatment. This will require more money and manpower and better use of beds, staff and equipment. For example, more surgery could be done on a day basis. There is also need for improved rehabilitation services and for the concentration of accident and emergency services.

Child Health Services

The Court Report has indicated the major improvements needed in the health services for children to bring them together into an integrated service. Not all children are assessed after birth for the early detection of handicap. In some places there are not enough special care facilities for low birth-weight and sick newborn babies. A major expansion in the work done by health visitors is needed.

The Mentally Ill

Many mentally ill people now in the old psychiatric hospitals could live in the community if all the local services were there to help them do so—including homes, hostels and centres where they can feel "at home" and rebuild contacts with families and friends. Only about one-third of districts provide a comprehensive psychiatric service in their general hospitals, only a fifth of the 30,000 places needed in day centres are provided and only a third of the 12,000 places needed in residential homes. Adequate accommodation for mentally infirm old people is sadly lacking.

The Mentally Handicapped

While it is now known that some forms of severe mental handicap could be prevented, the necessary services are not widely provided. Nor are the needs and capacities of every handicapped person carefully assessed at an early stage. The mentally handicapped do not yet receive all the education and training which could help them make the most of their abilities; nor do families with handicapped children get all the help they need. So far about a third of the 34,000 places needed in residential homes and only about half of the 73,000 places needed in training centres are provided. On top of this small hospital units are needed to replace low standard accommodation in large institutions. About 70 hospitals still have 200 or more beds. Local authorities have still a long way to go before their community services for the mentally ill and mentally handicapped are fully provided.

The Elderly

Much of the hospital accommodation used for elderly people is still in what were originally poor law infirmaries, tuberculosis sanatoria or other buildings converted from different uses. The continuing growth in the number of elderly people will add to the need for space and staff —in general hospitals, for the acutely ill, and in community hospitals for those needing longer term care. More elderly people could be looked after at home if community nursing and other services were expanded. There is also a special need for further development of chiropody services.

The Younger Disabled

Disabled adults who are under 65 would also benefit from an expansion in the community nursing and other services to help them live fuller lives in their own homes. Special hostels need to be developed for the deaf and mentally disturbed and for those who are both deaf and blind. More places are needed in day centres and in residential homes. Extra hospital provision is also needed for the younger disabled; and extra facilities are required for those suffering from spinal injuries.

Primary Care

The number of health visitors needs to be increased by 50 per cent to meet existing needs and many more nurses are needed in the community. Some parts of the country are still short of general practitioners and particularly in the inner city areas there are still many general practitioners who work alone and have only a tenuous relationship with the other community health services.

Conclusion

This catalogue of buildings which need replacement, of services which need to be redesigned or relocated and of gaps in what is currently provided should not overshadow the real achievements of the last thirty years. It is because there is a planning system that what seem now to be future requirements can be specified with some precision and it is possible to identify what still needs to be done as resources can be found to do it. It is one of the advantages of a National Health Service that new needs come to light and that better ways of meeting needs are constantly being identified. What are now thought to be the best ways of meeting particular needs may well cease to be appropriate in the coming decades in the light of new knowledge, new techniques and lessons learnt from local experiments or from experience abroad. The experience of 30 years has shown that plans have to be constantly revised. While trends can be identified, future needs and future ways of meeting them are far from being wholly predictable.

Britain is not alone in facing the twin challenges of rising expectations and of the extraordinary growth of medical technology over the past 30 years. All advanced societies are worried about the problem of paying for all the health care which could be provided. The problems faced by less developed countries in choosing their health priorities are even more formidable. What the National Health Service provides is an organisational structure within which priorities can be consciously chosen after widespread discussion with the professional interests at each level of the Service and of those who use it.

A Royal Commission on the National Health Service is currently at work. One of its tasks is to re-examine the organisation of the Service. This too may need to be adapted in years to come in response to wider changes in society and in the services which have to be planned and organised. New ways may be found through central and local political institutions of accommodating the differing interests of those working in the Service and those using it.

Faster progress could be made in doing what needs to be done if the burden falling on the National Health Service of preventable illness and accidents could be lightened—if people too more responsibility for safeguarding their own health rather than expecting health professionals to restore what has been thrown away. But the saving of health resources of many preventive actions comes only over a long period. And in the still longer run the Health Service needs of a health-conscious population may be more costly. The prevention of death of the young and middle-aged adds to the number of those who will eventually need costly care in old age. Cynics may say that the new international interest in the potentialities of preventive medicine is a response to falling rates of economic growth and inadequate resources of money and manpower available to be used to expand health and other services. If the economic situation has led to a tougher look to see where resources could be saved, this is all to the good. But what cannot be denied is that a substantial part of the Health Service is currently engaged in trying to repair the harm which people do to themselves and to each other which could readily be avoided. If current health resources have to be used in this way, they are not available to provide for those whose needs are not being fully met and who can in no way be held responsible for their need for health care. The adoption of healthier life styles would not save health care resources, but it could allow them to be used to meet more pressing needs and, with so much still to be done, that would reduce unnecessary suffering and help people to live fuller lives.

Appendix

Figure 1
**NHS current expenditure:
£ millions 1970 prices**   **United Kingdom**

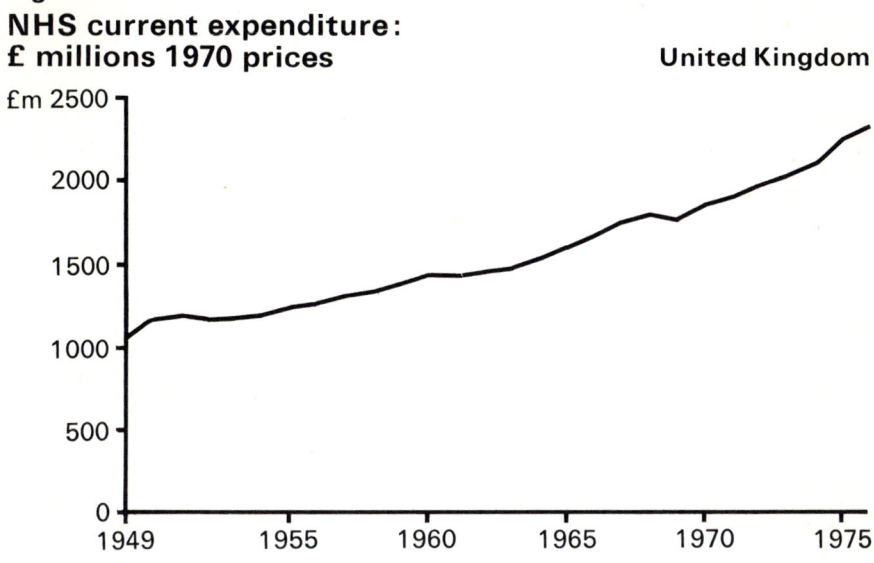

Source: CSO

Figure 2

**Total NHS expenditure as a percentage
of Gross Domestic Product**   **United Kingdom**

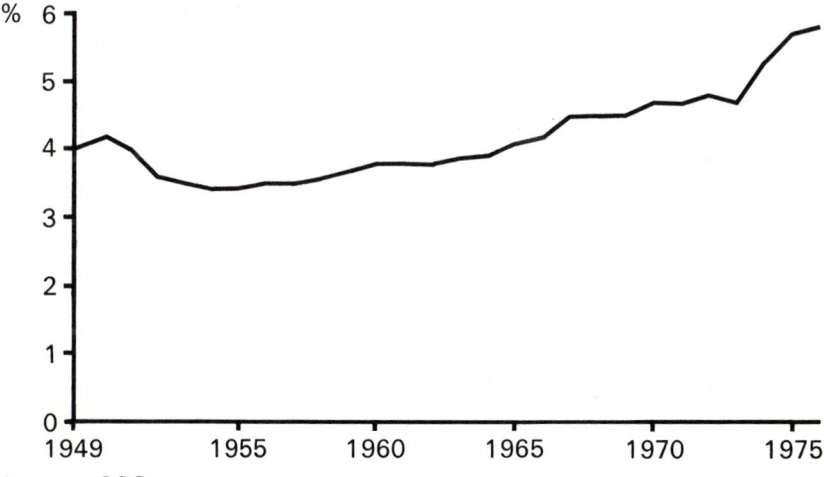

Source: CSO

Figure 3
Health centres –
numbers open at the end of the year   England and Wales

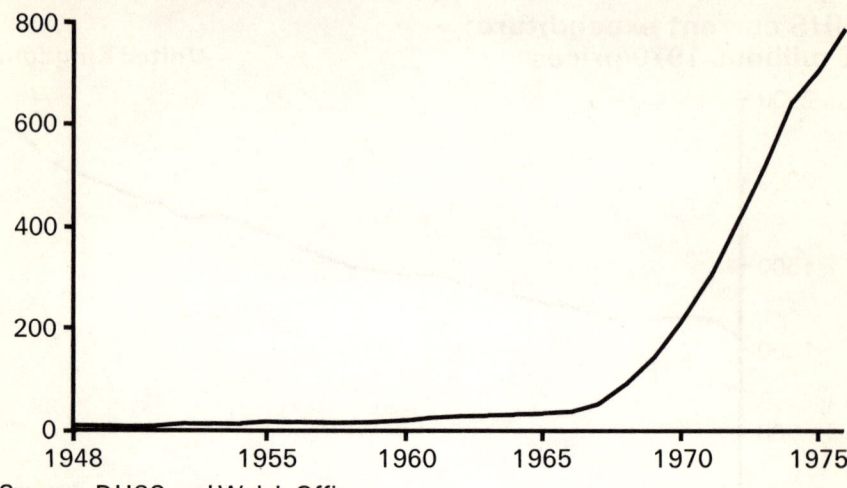

Source: DHSS and Welsh Office

Figure 4
NHS capital expenditure:
£ millions 1970 prices   United Kingdom

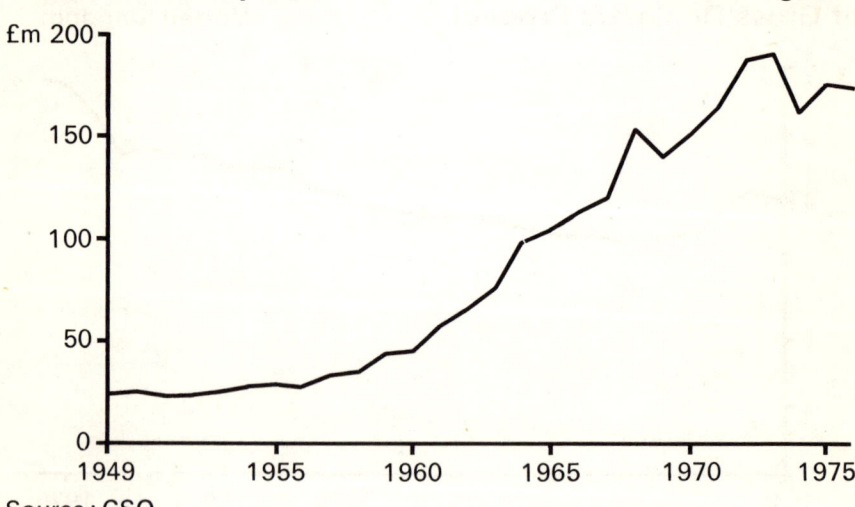

Source: CSO

Figure 5

NHS hospital manpower* – whole-time equivalents

England and Wales

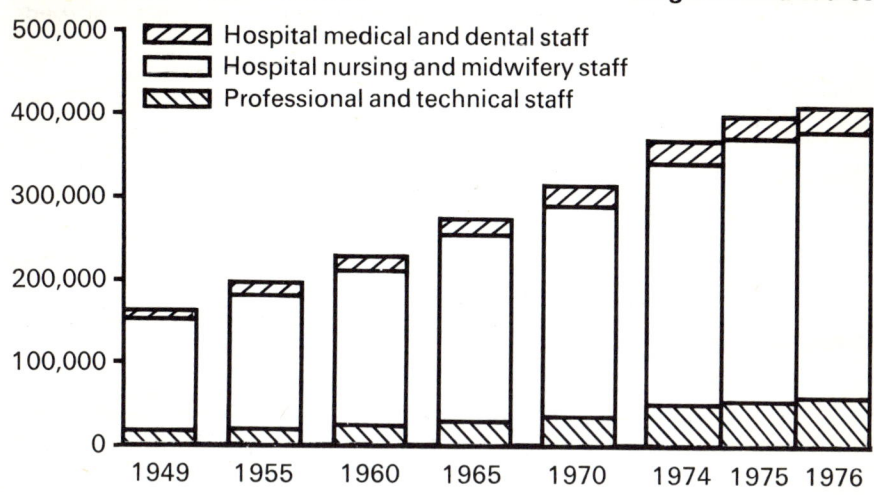

Source : DHSS and Welsh Office

*Figures for 1974–1976 for professional and technical staff relate to NHS staff

Figure 6

Community health nursing staff* – whole-time equivalents

England and Wales

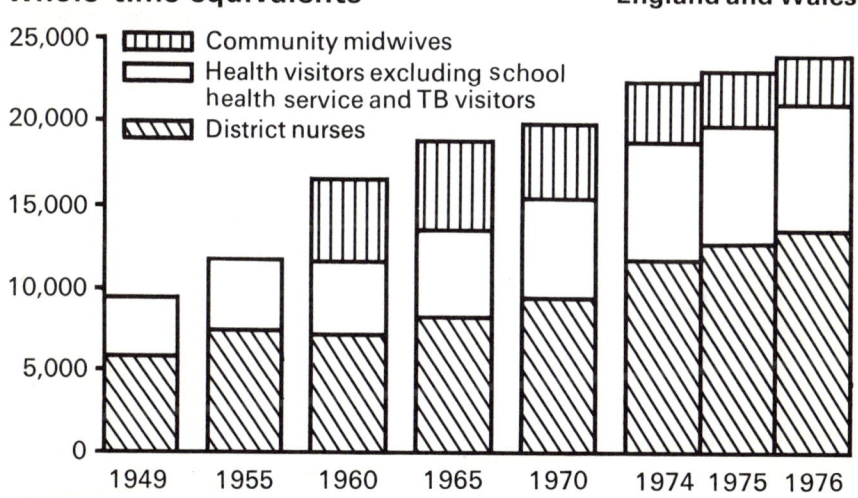

Source : DHSS and Welsh Office

*Figures for 1949 and 1955 for community midwives are not available

Figure 7

Occupied hospital beds

England and Wales

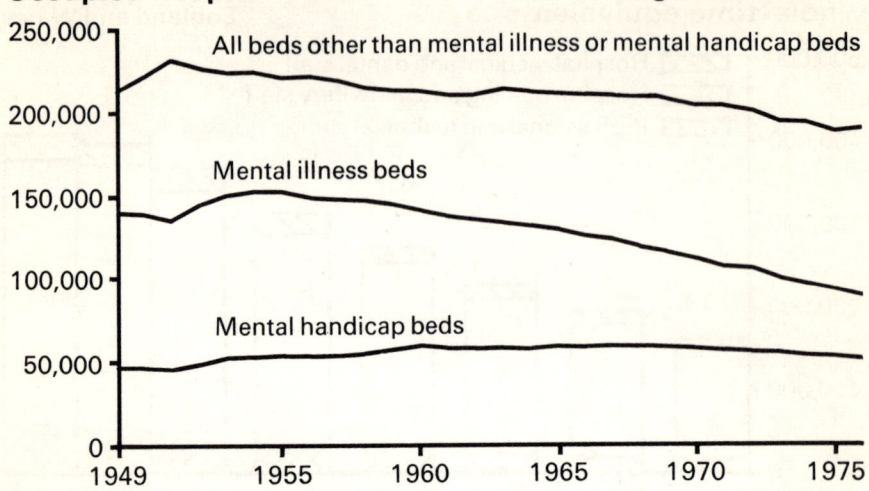

All beds other than mental illness or mental handicap beds

Mental illness beds

Mental handicap beds

Source : DHSS and Welsh Office

N.B. The figures for 1949–1957 are estimated

Figure 8

Hospital in-patients – discharges and deaths : millions

England and Wales

Source : DHSS and Welsh Office

Figure 9

Out-patient attendances including
accident and emergency: millions
England and Wales

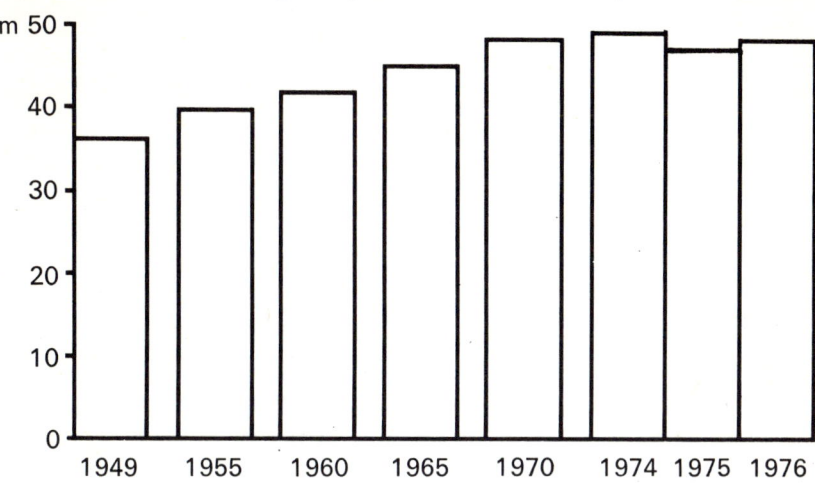

Source: DHSS and Welsh Office

Figure 10

Health visiting* –
number of persons seen: millions
England and Wales

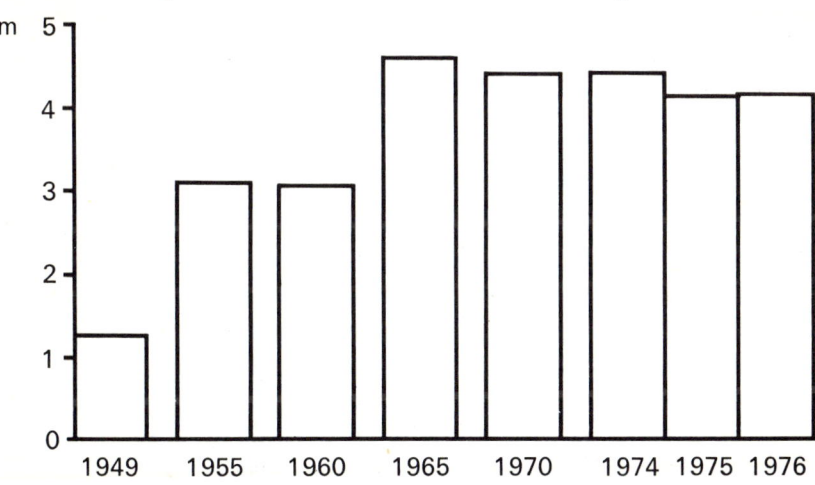

Source: DHSS and Welsh Office

*Because of a change of definition figures from 1974–6 are not comparable with earlier years

Figure 11
District nursing* –
number of persons treated : millions   **England and Wales**

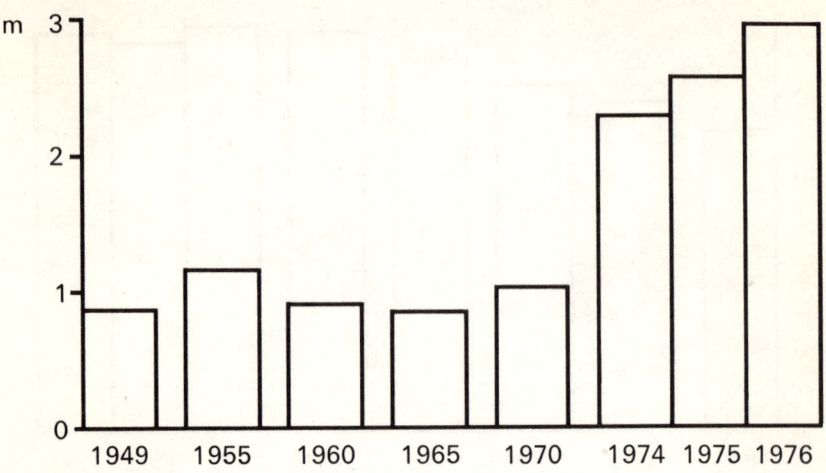

Source : DHSS and Welsh Office

*Because of a change of definition figures from 1974–6 are not comparable with earlier years

Figure 12
Domiciliary midwifery* – domiciliary confinements
and early discharge cases   **England and Wales**

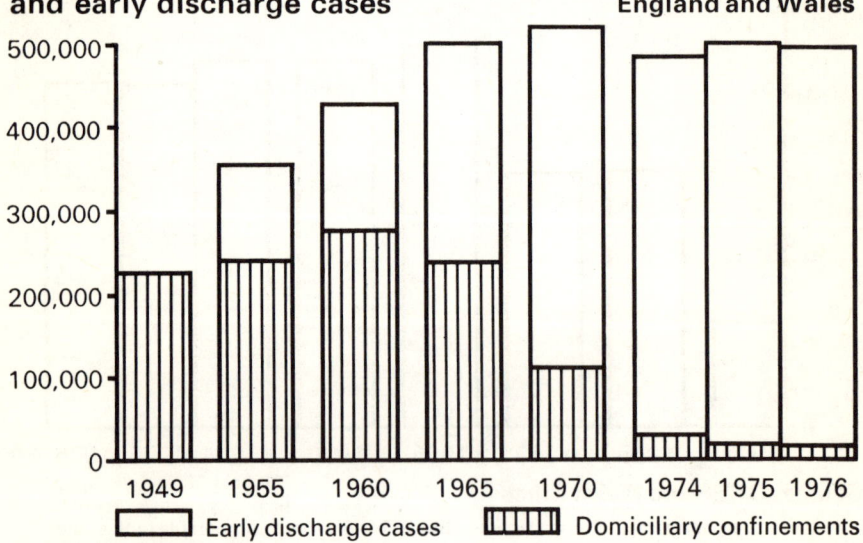

☐ Early discharge cases   ▥ Domiciliary confinements

Source : DHSS and Welsh Office

*1949 figure for early discharge cases is not available

Bibliography

Books:
1. Political and Economic Planning: *Report on the British Health Services*, PEP 1937.
2. Levy, Hermann, *National Health Insurance. A Critical Study*, Cambridge, 1944.
3. Aneurin Bevan. *In Place of Fear*, Heinemann, 1952 (New Edition, 1976).
4. Brian Abel-Smith and R. M. Titmuss. *The Cost of the National Health Service in England and Wales*, Cambridge, 1956.
5. Brian Abel-Smith. *A History of the Nursing Profession*, Heinemann, 1960.
6. Almont Lindsey. *Socialised Medicine in England and Wales: the National Health Service 1948–61*, University of North Carolina Press, 1962.
7. Brian Abel-Smith. *The Hospitals 1800–1948: a study in social administration in England and Wales*, Heinemann, 1964.
8. Willcocks, Arthur I. *The creation of the National Health Service: a study of pressure groups and a major social policy decision*, Routledge and Kegan Paul, 1967.
9. Michael Foot. *Aneurin Bevan: a biography*. Volume 2: 1945–60, Davis-Poynter, 1973.

Royal Commissions
1. *Report of the Royal Commission on the Law relating to Mental Illness and Mental Deficiency, 1954–57.* (Chairman: Lord Percy of Newcastle) HMSO, 1956: Cmnd. 169.
2. *Report of the Royal Commission on Doctors and Dentists Remuneration, 1957–60.* (Chairman: Sir Harry Pilkington) HMSO 1960: Cmnd. 939.
3. *Royal Commission on Local Government in Greater London, 1957–60.* (Chairman: Sir Edwin Herbert) HMSO 1960: Cmnd. 1164.
4. *Report of the Royal Commission on Medical Education, 1965–68.* (Chairman: Baron Todd) HMSO 1968: Cmnd. 3569.

5. *Report of the Royal Commission on Local Government in England, 1966–69*. (Chairman: the Rt Hon Lord Redcliffe Maud) HMSO 1969: Cmnd. 4040 (3 vols).
Local Government Reform—short version of report. HMSO 1969: Cmnd. 4039.

Official Committees

1. *Report of the Committee on the Internal Administration of Hospitals*. Committee of the Central Health Services Council. (Bradbeer Committee) HMSO 1954.
2. *Report of the Committee of Enquiry into the Cost of the National Health Service*. (Guillebaud Committee) HMSO 1956: Cmnd. 9663.
3. *Report of the Committee to Consider the Future Numbers of Medical Practitioners and the Appropriate Intake of Medical Students*. (Willink Report) HMSO 1957.
4. *Interim Report of the Committee on the Cost of Prescribing*. (Hinchcliffe Committee) HMSO 1958.
5. *Final Report of the Committee on the Cost of Prescribing*. (Hinchcliffe Committee) HMSO 1959.
6. *Report of the Maternity Services Committee*. (Cranbrook Report) HMSO 1959.
7. *Report of the Joint Working Party on the Medical Staffing Structure in the Hospital Service*. (Platt Report) HMSO 1961.
8. *Report of the Committee on Local Authority and Allied Personal Social Services*. (Seebohm Committee) HMSO 1968: Cmnd. 3703.
9. *Report of the Committee on Nursing*. (Briggs Report) HMSO 1972: Cmnd. 5115.

White Papers

1. Ministry of Health and Department of Health for Scotland. *A National Health Service*. HMSO 1944: Cmnd. 6502.
2. DHSS. *Better Services for the Mentally Handicapped*. HMSO 1971: Cmnd. 4683.
3. DHSS. *National Health Service Reorganisation: England*. HMSO 1972: Cmnd. 5055.
4. Welsh Office. *National Health Service Reorganisation in Wales*. HMSO 1972: Cmnd. 5057.
5. DHSS. *Better Services for the Mentally Ill*. HMSO 1965: Cmnd. 6233.

Green Papers and Consultative Documents

1. DHSS and Welsh Office. *The Administrative Structure of the medical and related services in England and Wales*. HMSO 1968 (Green Paper).

2. DHSS. *The Future Structure of the National Health Service.* HMSO 1970 (Green Paper).
3. Welsh Office. *Reorganisation of the National Health Service in Wales.* HMSO 1970 (Green Paper).
4. DHSS. *National Health Service Reorganisation: Consultative Document.* HMSO 1971.
5. DHSS. *Consultative Document—Prevention and Health: Everybody's Business.* A reassessment of public and personal health. HMSO 1976.
6. DHSS. *Consultative Document—Priorities in the Health and Personal Social Services.* HMSO 1976.
7. DHSS. *Priorities in the Health and Social Services: The Way Forward.* HMSO 1977.

Official Reports etc.
Annual Reports:
> *Report of the Ministry of Health/Department of Health and Social Security.*
> *On the State of the Public Health:* Report of the Chief Medical Officer.

1. Ministry of Health. *Distribution of Remuneration among General Practitioners.* (Danckwerts Award) HMSO 1952: Cmnd. 8599.
2. Ministry of Health. *The Hospital Plan for England and Wales.* HMSO 1962: Cmnd. 1604.
3. Ministry of Health. *Health and Welfare: the Development of Community Care.* HMSO 1963: Cmnd. 1973.
4. Ministry of Health. *The Hospital Building Programme:* A revision of the Hospital Plan for England and Wales. HMSO 1966: Cmnd. 3000.
5. *The Family Doctor Service.* Joint Reports of Discussions between General Practitioners' Representatives and the Minister of Health, 1965–66. Ministry of Health and British Medical Association, 1966.
6. *Report of the Committee of Inquiry into Allegations of Ill-Treatment of Patients and other irregularities at the Ely Hospital, Cardiff.* HMSO 1969: Cmnd. 3975.
7. Government Social Survey, 1970. *Adult Dental Health in England and Wales in 1968.* HMSO 1970.
8. *Report of the Farleigh Hospital Committee of Inquiry.* HMSO 1971: Cmnd. 4557.
9. *Report of the Committee of Inquiry into Whittingham Hospital.* HMSO 1972: Cmnd. 4861.

10. DHSS. *Management arrangements for the Reorganised National Health Service* (Grey Book). Report of the Management Study Steering Committee (Chairman: Sir Philip Rogers). HMSO 1972.
11. DHSS and Welsh Office. *Reorganisation of the National Health Service and local government in England and Wales:* A report from the Working Party on collaboration between the National Health Service and local government on its activities to the end of 1972 (Chairman: A. R. W. Bavin). HMSO 1972.

    A report . . . from January to July 1973.

    A report . . . from July 1973 to April 1974. HMSO 1974.
12. DHSS. *Allocations to Regions in 1976–77:* First Interim Report of the Resource Allocation Working Party. DHSS 1975.
13. DHSS. *Sharing Resources for Health in England:* Report of the Resource Allocation Working Party. HMSO 1976.

Unofficial Reports
1. *A Review of the medical services in Great Britain:* The Report of the Medical Services Review Committee (Porritt Committee). Social Assay, 1962.
2. *A Charter for the Family Doctor Service.* British Medical Association 1965.

Printed for Her Majesty's Stationery Office by UDO (Litho) Ltd., London
Dd. 587178 K16 8/78